By the Editors of Consumer Guide®

Auto Tune-Ups Made Easy

BEEKMAN HOUSE
NEW YORK

Contents

Manufactured in the United States of America
1 2 3 4 5 6 7 8 9 10

Library of Congress Catalog Card Number: 79-2434
ISBN: 0-517-292890

This edition published by:
Beekman House
A Division of Crown Publishers, Inc.
One Park Avenue
New York, N.Y. 10016

Cover Design: Frank E. Peiler
Illustrations: Steven Boswick
Consultant: Robert R. Duncan, SAE, Coordinator, Automotive Technology Apprenticeship Program, Oakton Community College, Morton Grove, Illinois

Contents

Servicing the Fuel System 23

Good carburetion service is mainly directed at the carburetor, but other fuel system components also need inspection and maintenance.

Servicing the Ignition System 37

After you've inspected, cleaned, and tested the battery, the main electrical components left to be serviced in a basic tune-up are the spark plugs and the distributor.

Adjusting the Carburetor 82

Carburetor adjustments are basically intended to correct two minor faults, but they are important steps to every complete engine tune-up.

Final Tune-Up Steps 90

Quick-Reference Maintenance and Lubrication Guide................. 91

Glossary 93

Tuning Your Car

Every car, whether it's 10 years old or brand new, needs to be tuned periodically to keep running efficiently. You can tell when a tune-up is required by such symptoms as an increase in fuel consumption, a definite lack of pep, rough idling or difficult starting. You can't expect a car with an out-of-tune engine to give you good gas mileage. Such a vehicle not only robs you of the peak performance you expect, but also costs you money by wasting fuel.

Professional car maintenance and repair is costly. And, it's getting costlier all the time. For example, an engine tune-up that may cost $70 or more at a professional garage can be self-performed by you for about $25. It also can be inconvenient. By doing the work yourself, you can do it at your own convenience, eliminating the need to get on a service station's "waiting list."

There are other benefits. If you don't know how your car functions, you are at a serious disadvantage in dealing with a mechanic. By doing your own tune-ups, you'll become familiar with your vehicle; so, when you do encounter a repair that must be done by a professional, you'll probably know what needs to be done and will be able to discuss it intelligently with the mechanic. In this way, you can avoid costly and often needless servicing.

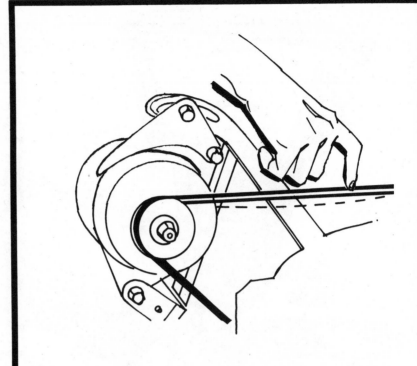

A tune-up is a good opportunity to perform a number of other checks and services. For example, the drive belt must be properly tensioned. There should be no more than 3/4 inch of deflection when you press the belt down with your finger.

There's another good reason for the do-it-yourself approach. Even routine maintenance, such as an oil change, is disappearing from the list of services offered by neighborhood stations. Many are becoming places where you can buy only gasoline.

The First Tune-Up. Your first tune-up will probably be the most time-consuming, especially if you are not familiar with your car's engine. But you'll find that it's not that difficult. So, for your first effort, it's best to allow a full day. The second time you do it, the job will be much easier and should only take you a few hours. For one thing, you'll know which tools are necessary. For example, an ordinary open-end wrench may not be adequate to loosen a distributor's hold-down bolt if the bolt is difficult to reach on your car. You may need a special distributor wrench for this task.

Before beginning your first tune-up, read this book from cover to cover to familiarize yourself with the

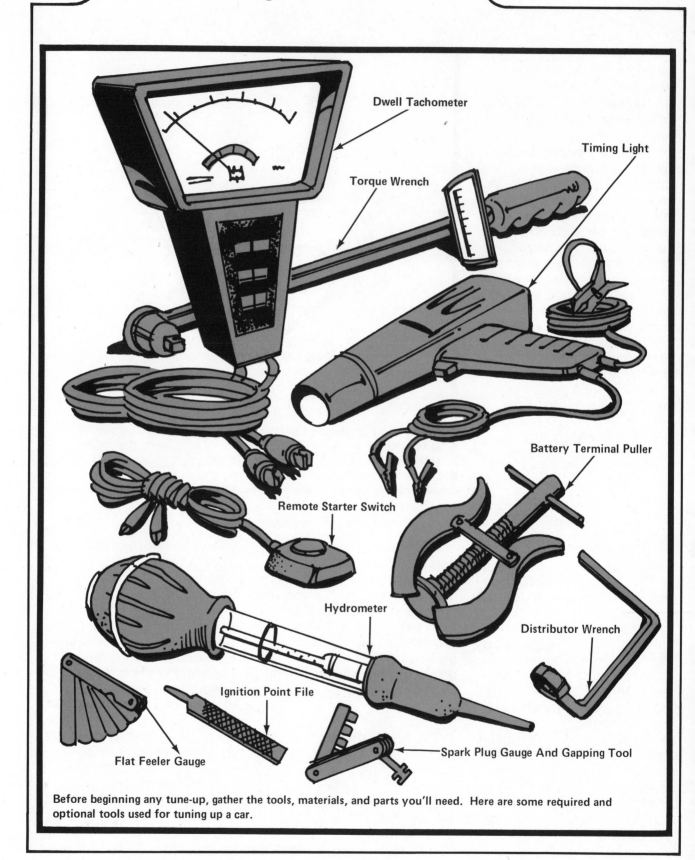

Dwell Tachometer

Timing Light

Torque Wrench

Battery Terminal Puller

Remote Starter Switch

Hydrometer

Distributor Wrench

Ignition Point File

Flat Feeler Gauge

Spark Plug Gauge And Gapping Tool

Before beginning any tune-up, gather the tools, materials, and parts you'll need. Here are some required and optional tools used for tuning up a car.

main tune-up steps. Check to see which ones apply to your car and which do not. This also applies to tools and replacement parts.

Tools, Materials, and Parts. Before beginning the tune-up, it's a good idea to make sure everything is handy. On the right is a checklist of tools, materials, and parts you'll most likely need for your tune-up.

Read Your Manual. Once you've determined which replacement parts you will need, check the owner's or service manual for your car to make certain that you buy the proper replacement parts. Then, purchase the items *before* starting.

The owner's manual contains a wealth of information about your car. If you haven't done so lately, now's a good time to reread it and refresh your memory. In addition to giving operating instructions for your car, it lists specifications for such items as lamps, fuses, fluids, spark plugs, filters, and tire pressure. Late-model cars also contain important data on a label under the hood. You'll need to know this information for the tune-up.

A basic tune-up, however, mainly concerns the car's ignition system and carburetor. It involves cleaning and replacing some components, making a number of adjustments, and

Tools
- ☐ Extension work light
- ☐ Wheel chocks
- ☐ Safety goggles
- ☐ Screwdrivers
- ☐ Pliers
- ☐ Open-end wrenches
- ☐ Flare-nut or tubing wrench
- ☐ Torque wrench (optional)
- ☐ Hexagonal Allen wrench
- ☐ Wire brush
- ☐ Penknife (optional)
- ☐ Remote starter switch (optional)
- ☐ Jumper wire (optional)
- ☐ Flat feeler gauge
- ☐ Ignition point file
- ☐ Spark plug socket, extension, and ratchet wrench
- ☐ Spark plug boot puller (optional)
- ☐ Spark plug gap gauge (round wire) and gapping tool
- ☐ Hose clamp pliers
- ☐ Distributor wrench (optional)
- ☐ Battery terminal puller
- ☐ Battery terminal cleaning tool (optional)
- ☐ Hydrometer
- ☐ Dwell tachometer (optional)
- ☐ Timing light

Materials
- ☐ Masking tape
- ☐ Pencil
- ☐ Clean cloths
- ☐ Solvent (kerosene)
- ☐ Cam lubricant
- ☐ Golf tees
- ☐ Motor oil
- ☐ Chalk
- ☐ Baking soda
- ☐ Water
- ☐ Penetrating oil
- ☐ Steel wool
- ☐ Petroleum jelly
- ☐ Sandpaper
- ☐ Distilled water
- ☐ Toothpicks
- ☐ Carburetor cleaner
- ☐ Metal containers
- ☐ Small paintbrush
- ☐ Household thermometer

Parts
- ☐ Spark plugs
- ☐ Points and condenser
- ☐ Air cleaner filter element
- ☐ Fuel filter
- ☐ PCV valve
- ☐ PCV filter

conducting a series of checks or tests. A tune-up is also a good opportunity to perform some other jobs. In fact, some of these tasks should be done every time you raise the hood of your car. They include visual checks for defects or damage in hoses, belts, and wiring.

The tune-up procedure in this book includes an inspection and test of the battery. But a tune-up is a good time to routinely check the car's other fluids, including the radiator coolant, brake fluid, power steering fluid, engine oil, and automatic transmission fluid. If you don't know how to make such checks, your owner's manual will tell you.

If you decide to do the tune-up outdoors, pick a day with nice weather for the job and park on a level site. If you work in a garage, make sure that there's adequate cross-ventilation, because

you'll be running the engine. An extension work light, even if you work outside, will be invaluable.

Use the proper tools for the job. Never hammer anything that proves to be stubborn. If a fastener refuses to budge or is difficult to remove, apply a little penetrating oil and allow it time to work. And, when you remove parts, arrange them in the order of removal and place them in a tray or other container so they won't get lost. This will

also ease reassembly.

If your car has an automatic transmission, put the gear lever in "park." With manual transmission, place the gear lever in "neutral." On both types of cars, engage the parking brake and block the drive wheels with wheel chocks. Then, raise the hood and place drop cloths over the car's front fenders to protect the paint finish from dropped tools and harmful fluids.

Now, you're ready to begin. . . .

Before working on your vehicle, engage the parking brake and block the drive wheels with wheel chocks. It's a good idea to place drop cloths over both front fenders to protect the car's finish.

Servicing the Battery

Keeping your car's battery clean and in good working order is one of the most essential services you can do and it's one of the easiest.

On every battery, there is a positive and negative terminal or connector. If a wire were to be placed across these two terminals, you would have a short circuit and plenty of sparks. A wire is a superb conductor of electricity. But dust and dirt are conductors of electricity too, especially when they are damp. Without realizing it, you can have a fine, nearly invisible conductor of electricity on a

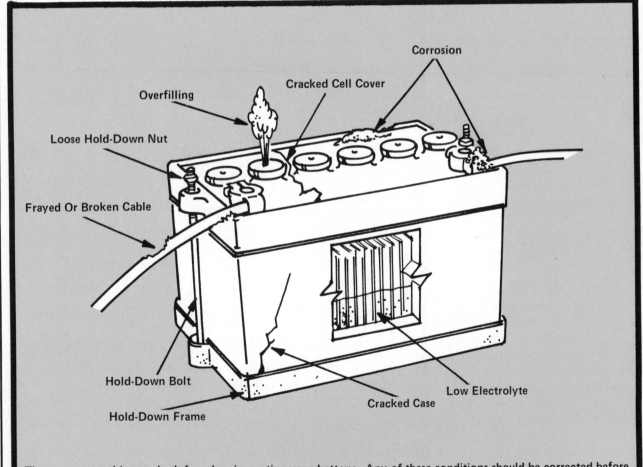

There are many things to look for when inspecting your battery. Any of these conditions should be corrected before you service or test the battery.

dirty battery that slowly bleeds away your battery's power. It is not strong enough to create sparks, but nevertheless, the "leakage" is there.

Another, and more common, power loss is through poor connections to the battery terminals. We're all familiar with the buildup of whitish-green corrosion that accumulates on battery terminals. This substance is the result of the chemical action due to gases coming from the inside of the battery. This corrosion is an excellent insulator and often forms between the battery cable and the terminal. The outside of the connection may look good, but inside there's just enough corrosion to prevent electricity from flowing.

Inspecting the Battery. A thorough battery inspection should be done at least twice a year, and it can be easily performed during an engine tune-up. Your battery inspection should include the following:

1. Check the battery electrolyte level. It should be above the tops of the plates or at the indicated level within the cells. Add water to bring the electrolyte to the correct level. Don't overfill. If you have a maintenance-free battery, check its indicator to determine its condition.
2. Inspect the battery case and cover for dirt or

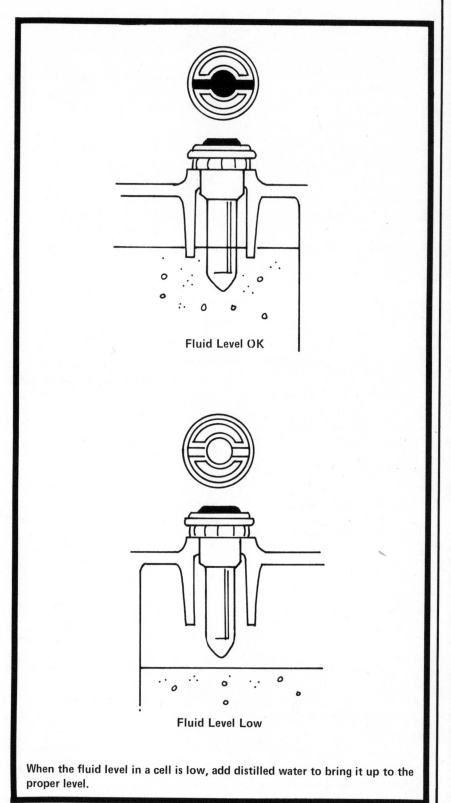

Fluid Level OK

Fluid Level Low

When the fluid level in a cell is low, add distilled water to bring it up to the proper level.

grease that could cause a voltage leak to ground.

3. Inspect the battery terminals, cable connectors, and metal parts of the hold-down and tray for signs of acid corrosion.
4. Inspect the battery for cracks, loose terminal posts and other physical damage. A battery with this kind of damage is ready for replacement.
5. Check for missing or damaged cell caps. Replace any that are defective or missing.
6. Inspect the cables for broken wire strands, worn insulation, and loose or damaged connectors. Replace defective cables.
7. Check all cable connections for looseness and dirt.
8. Inspect the tray and hold-down for looseness, damage or missing parts.
9. Make sure that heat shields are properly installed on batteries requiring them.

Cleaning the Battery. During the battery inspection and tune-up, it should be cleaned. For this task, you'll need the following: masking tape, baking soda, water, clean cloths, penetrating oil (optional), steel wool or a stiff wire brush, sandpaper, petroleum jelly, wrenches or battery pliers, a battery terminal puller, penknife (optional), and a battery terminal cleaning tool

(optional). Here's how to clean your battery:

1. Wear old clothes. The substance that you use to clean off a dirty battery contains strong acid. Don't let it touch your skin, and if it does, be sure to wash it off immediately. **CAUTION:** Don't smoke or tackle this job in the vicinity of an open flame. Batteries can be highly explosive due to hydrogen gas.
2. Be sure the vent caps, if any, are in place on the battery and cover the vent holes in the caps with masking tape to avoid getting cleaning solution in the battery. You don't want to neutralize the acid that makes the battery work.
3. In about a pint of water, pour enough baking soda to get a strong solution. It should fizz. Pour this on the battery top and wait until the foaming stops. Remember, don't allow the soda solution to enter the battery. Scrub the top of the battery with a stiff brush. Then rinse the battery off with plenty of fresh water. Dry the battery.

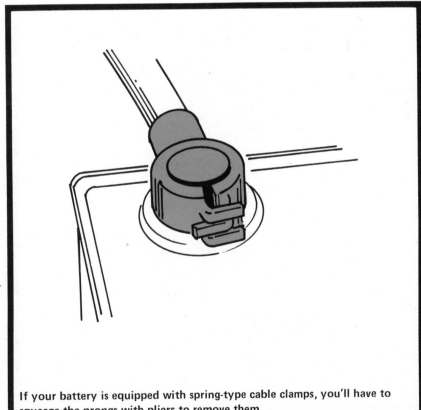

If your battery is equipped with spring-type cable clamps, you'll have to squeeze the prongs with pliers to remove them.

4. Remove the battery cable clamps. Begin by removing the ground cable first. On most batteries, this is done by loosening a nut and bolt with a wrench. But if your battery is equipped with spring-type cable clamps, you'll have to squeeze the prongs with pliers. Use a terminal puller to lift off the clamp. In either case, remove the ground cable first. This is the negative (–) terminal on most cars. If the positive cable is disconnected first, you could accidentally ground the wrench or pliers against the body or some other part of the car and create a spark. (On cars with positive ground systems, remove the positive cable first.) **CAUTION:** There is the possibility of exploding the battery, ruining the wrench or burning your hand with the heavy current flow. Always follow the instructions to be safe.

Because of the highly corrosive nature of battery acid, you may find that the cable clamp nuts have been so eaten away that they are virtually impossible to remove. In this case, you may have to apply some penetrating oil for a while until whatever remains of the nut can be turned. This is a good case for owning a battery terminal puller; sometimes the cable clamp is too corroded for normal measures. If so, it is advisable to replace the cable when the job is finished or at least to replace the clamp if the wire in the cable is still good. Avoid putting a new clamp on a wire where the insulation is bad or where too many strands of wire have deteriorated. **NOTE:** Most late-model General Motors cars have side terminal batteries. These terminals are less likely to corrode but still should be checked periodically and cleaned if necessary.

5. When both cable clamps are removed, use a wire

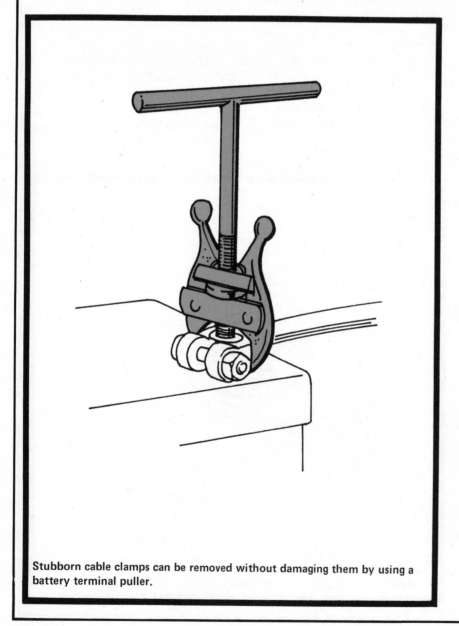

Stubborn cable clamps can be removed without damaging them by using a battery terminal puller.

Terminal Cap

Many late-model cars have side terminal batteries. These terminals are less likely to corrode but still should be checked and cleaned if necessary.

brush or steel wool to clean the battery terminals and clamps until they are shiny. The inside of the clamps can be cleaned with sandpaper or lightly scraped with a penknife. A good investment is a battery terminal cleaning tool. This tool can be bought in kit combinations that include the terminal puller and battery pliers. The terminal cleaner has a round "female" brush that is slipped over the

A battery terminal and clamp cleaner is a handy tool.

battery terminal and twisted to remove all traces of corrosion. On the other side of the brush is a "male" end that slips inside the battery cable clamp. Instead of using a penknife, a few twists of this brush removes the corrosion.

6. Replace the clamps on the battery, making sure they fit well down onto the terminals. Connect the insulated (hot) cable to the battery first, and then the ground cable. Don't hammer the clamp down or overtighten the nut because this could damage the battery case or the clamp. If the old nuts are in bad condition, they should be replaced with a special type that can be obtained at your auto parts store.

Testing the Battery.
Because the starting system of a car is engineered to operate with a battery that is fully charged, a battery hydrometer is an indispensable tool for checking a battery's performance. The hydrometer compares the density (specific gravity or weight) of the battery fluid to that of water. The acid in your battery is heavier than plain water. Therefore, the more fully charged your battery, the heavier the fluid. This, of course, is the tip-off to the degree of charge in your battery. The "heavier" the fluid, the higher the

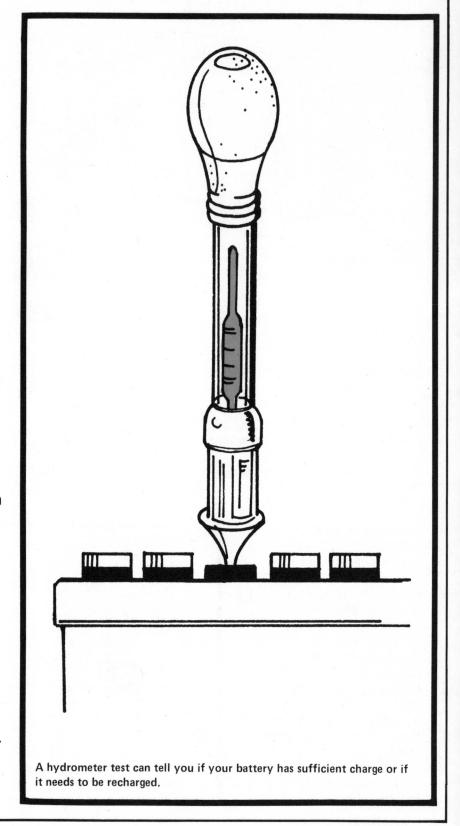

A hydrometer test can tell you if your battery has sufficient charge or if it needs to be recharged.

The Battery

degree of charge.

A hydrometer test of your battery should be made seasonally or during a tune-up to avoid strain on the car's electrical system as well as to detect battery trouble before it fails. For this, you'll need a hydrometer, distilled water, and some toothpicks. To perform the hydrometer or specific gravity test, follow these steps:

1. With the engine off, remove the vent caps and check the fluid level of the battery. If there isn't enough fluid in the cells to allow you to take a good sampling of fluid with the hydrometer, you will have to add distilled water. If this is the case, run your engine for approximately 20 minutes to let the fresh water mix thoroughly with the fluid already in the battery. Then stop the engine and let the car cool for 15 minutes before performing the hydrometer test.

2. Test each cell of the battery with the hydrometer, one at a time. Suck enough battery fluid into the hydrometer with the attached rubber bulb to float the indicator inside the tube and take a reading. On a bulb float-type tester, you'll get a false reading if the indicator touches the sides or the top of the instrument.

A reading from 1.260 to 1.300 in each cell means the battery is healthy. A consistent reading of approximately 1.225 probably means the battery is satisfactory but low on charge. Any cell that varies more than 0.050 from the others indicates a defective cell, and the battery should be replaced.

The specific gravity of a fully charged battery should be between 1.260 and 1.280, with the electrolyte temperature at 80°F. The accompanying illustrations depict the relationship between specific gravity and state of charge.

If the electrolyte temperature is above or below 80°F., the specific gravity reading must be corrected by *adding* 0.004 for each 10° above 80°F. or *subtracting* 0.004 for each 10° below 80°F. Here are two examples of temperature-corrected hydrometer readings:

Example No. 1: The indicator reading is 1.230, and the temperature reading is 10°F. The temperature must be corrected for a variation of 70°, or 28 points ($0.004 \times 7 = 0.028$) must be subtracted from the indicator reading of 1.230. The true corrected reading is 1.202.

Example No. 2: The indicator reading is 1.235, and the temperature reading is 120°F. Since the temperature reading is 40° above the standard of 80°F.,

16 points ($0.004 \times 4 = 0.016$) must be added to the indicator reading of 1.235. The true corrected reading is 1.251.

A battery should be recharged when the specific gravity drops below 1.230. A specific-gravity variation of more than 0.050 between cells indicates a battery that should be replaced.

If you have a battery tester that uses floating balls to indicate the battery's state of charge, draw in some battery fluid and observe the floating action. If all three balls are floating, the battery is fully charged; with two balls floating, the battery condition is fair; one floating ball means a poor state of charge; and no floating balls indicates a discharged battery.

3. Now check the battery vent caps and clean any plugged or dirty holes with a toothpick. This will help prevent acid fumes from building up dangerously in the battery. **NOTE:** Under normal driving conditions and weather conditions, a battery will lose up to two ounces of its fluid every 1,000 miles. If the fluid loss is greater than this amount, other parts of the car's charging system should be checked. Maintenance-free batteries are designed in such a way that they don't lose any fluid.

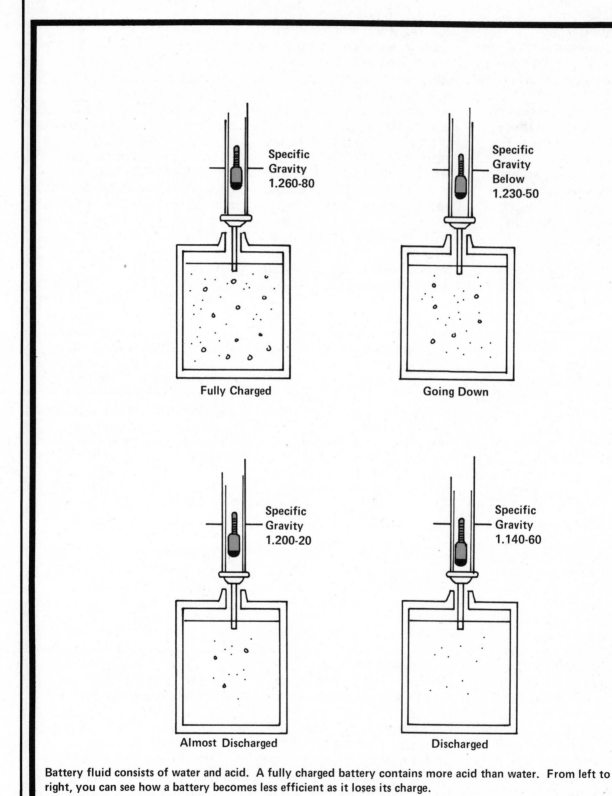

Specific Gravity 1.260-80

Fully Charged

Specific Gravity Below 1.230-50

Going Down

Specific Gravity 1.200-20

Almost Discharged

Specific Gravity 1.140-60

Discharged

Battery fluid consists of water and acid. A fully charged battery contains more acid than water. From left to right, you can see how a battery becomes less efficient as it loses its charge.

Servicing the PCV System

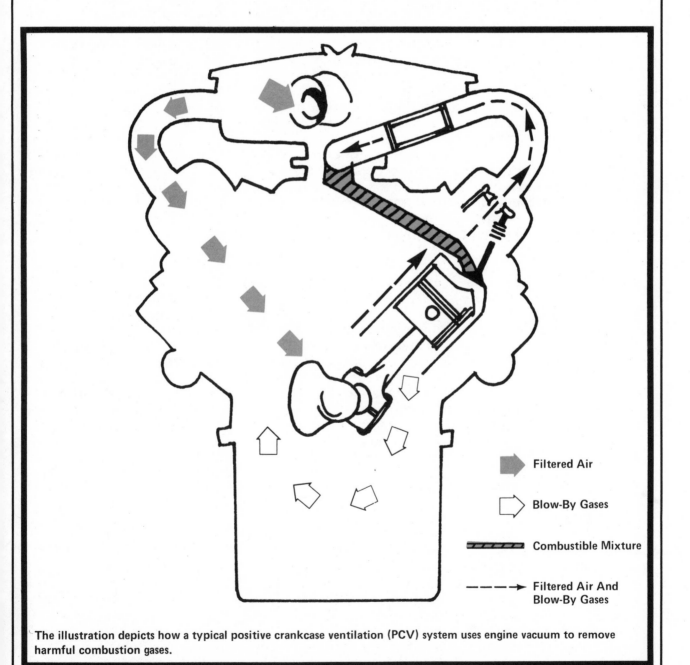

Filtered Air

Blow-By Gases

Combustible Mixture

Filtered Air And Blow-By Gases

The illustration depicts how a typical positive crankcase ventilation (PCV) system uses engine vacuum to remove harmful combustion gases.

The PCV System

As your automobile operates and the combustion process is taking place, a highly corrosive gas is produced. In addition, for every gallon of gasoline burned, more than a gallon of water is formed. During the last part of the engine's combustion stroke, some unburned fuel and products of combustion, such as water vapor, for instance, leak past the engine's piston rings into the crankcase. This leakage is the result of four things:

1. High pressures in the engine combustion chamber. This condition is created by the normal compression stroke in the engine under operation.
2. The necessary working clearance of piston rings in their grooves. Without this normal ring clearance, the engine's piston rings would not have room to expand from heat created by normal engine operation and seal properly against the cylinder walls.
3. The normal shifting of piston rings in their grooves that sometimes lines up the clearance gaps of two or more rings. This, too, is a normal condition. As the piston rings continue to turn in their grooves, the situation will correct itself.
4. The reduction in piston ring sealing contact area as the piston moves up and down in the cylinder.

This leakage into the engine crankcase often is referred to as "blow-by." This blow-by must be removed from the engine before it condenses in the crankcase and reacts with oil to form sludge. If sludge does form and is allowed to circulate with the engine oil, it will corrode and accelerate the wear of pistons, piston rings, valves, bearings and other internal working parts of the engine.

Complete burning of the air/fuel mixture in the engine never occurs, so blow-by carries a certain amount of unburned fuel from the engine's combustion chamber into the crankcase. If this unburned fuel is not removed, the oil in the crankcase will be diluted. And, oil diluted with gasoline will not lubricate the engine properly, causing excessive wear.

The combustion gases that do enter the engine crankcase are removed from the crankcase by means of a system using engine vacuum to draw fresh air through the crankcase. This system is called Positive Crankcase Ventilation (PCV).

This fresh air, which dissipates the harmful gases, enters through the air cleaner on top of the carburetor or through a separate PCV breather filter located on the inside of the carburetor air cleaner housing.

Since the vacuum supply for the PCV system is from the engine's intake manifold, the air flow through this system must be controlled in such a way that it varies in proportion to the regular air/fuel ratio being drawn into the intake manifold through the carburetor. Otherwise, the additional air being drawn into the system would cause the air/fuel mixture to become too lean for efficient engine operation.

The air flow through the PCV system into the intake manifold is regulated by the PCV valve. This valve, along with the necessary piping (metal tubing or rubber hose) and the intake breather filter, comprise the PCV system.

The PCV valve varies the amount of air flow through the system according to engine operation such as idle, cruise, acceleration, etc. The PCV valve itself consists of a coil spring, a valve, and a two-piece body that is crimped together. The valve dimensions, spring tension, and internal dimensions vary according to the engine they are used on to produce the desired air flow requirements. For this reason, when replacing a PCV valve, it is important to get a valve that is specifically designed for your car's engine.

The PCV system has three major benefits. It eliminates harmful crankcase gases by rerouting them through the intake manifold. It also reduces air pollution by not

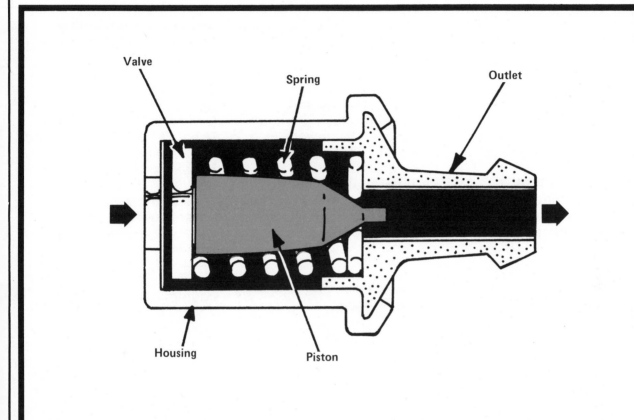

This is a cross-section of a PCV valve which is used to regulate the air flow into the intake manifold. This valve along with the necessary metal tubing or rubber hose and the intake breather filter comprise the PCV system.

allowing these gases to enter the atmosphere. And, it promotes fuel economy. The recirculated gases in the system are a combustible mixture. In effect, it becomes fuel for the engine when added to the air/fuel mixture entering the intake manifold from the carburetor.

Consequently, an inoperative PCV system could shorten the life of the engine by allowing harmful blow-by gases to remain in the engine, causing

corrosion and accelerating wear.

Car makers may vary on their recommendations for PCV system servicing and PCV valve replacement. But, as a general rule, you should check the PCV system for satisfactory operation every 12 months or 12,000 miles of driving, whichever comes first. Also, the PCV valve should be replaced at least every 24 months or 24,000 miles of driving, whichever comes first.

If you operate your car

under dusty conditions, subject your engine to long periods of idling or make mostly short trips in cold weather, you should check your PCV system more often.

You may be having trouble with your PCV system if you have a rough-running engine at idle speed, discover oil in the air cleaner housing, find oil leaks at any of the PCV system hose or tube connections or see oil leaks around the engine. Also, when you check the oil level of your engine and find that it is sludged up or appears to be diluted with gasoline (you can smell it) you probably have problems with the PCV system.

For servicing the PCV system, you'll need the following: pliers or screwdriver, wrench, motor oil, and cleaning solution.

Checking the PCV System. If you experience any of the symptoms described, a check of the PCV system is in order. **NOTE:** Before you replace a PCV valve or hoses, look over the entire system. Locate the hoses in the system and locate the PCV valve. You will see that one hose is connected to the carburetor air cleaner housing and to the engine at the valve cover. This hose carries filtered air from the carburetor air cleaner to the engine crankcase. It seldom needs service, other than making sure the connections are secure. The line formed by this hose is unrestricted and never contains the PCV valve.

Next, you'll see a hose connected between the engine valve cover and a fitting at the intake manifold just below the carburetor hose. The PCV valve will be installed as part of this line. Usually, the PCV valve will be installed in the end of the hose at the engine valve cover. However, the PCV valve will always be located somewhere in this line. Because the crankcase vapors and other contaminants are being drawn through the PCV valve and hose into the intake manifold, system problems are usually confined to this area.

Some rubber hoses have hose clamps requiring pliers or a screwdriver to loosen or tighten them. Most hose connections, however, simply slip over the PCV valve or connection at the intake manifold.

Start the engine and listen for vacuum leaks in the PCV system hose. If there is a leak, you will hear a slight hissing sound. Stop the engine. Inspect the hoses for cracks or any sign of deterioration. Since the PCV system must be airtight to operate efficiently, a leaking hose must be replaced. To replace a hose:

1. Disconnect the hose at both ends using either a screwdriver or pliers if the hose is secured with

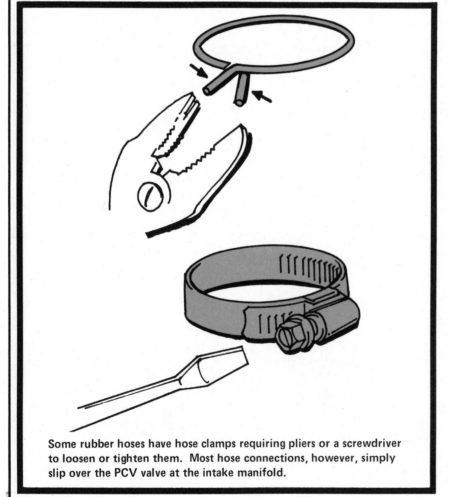

Some rubber hoses have hose clamps requiring pliers or a screwdriver to loosen or tighten them. Most hose connections, however, simply slip over the PCV valve at the intake manifold.

a hose clamp. If no clamp is used, simply pull the hose away from its connection. Remove the hose.

2. Purchase a length of PCV system hose from your auto supply store. Tell the person behind the counter the make and model car you are working on. In this way, he will be able to give you the correct diameter hose. Or, take the old hose with you and buy only the length that you need.

3. Using a sharp knife, cut the new hose to the same length as the one you removed.

4. Install the new PCV system hose, reversing Step 1.

Testing the PCV Valve. Having visually checked out the PCV system and having replaced any defective hose,

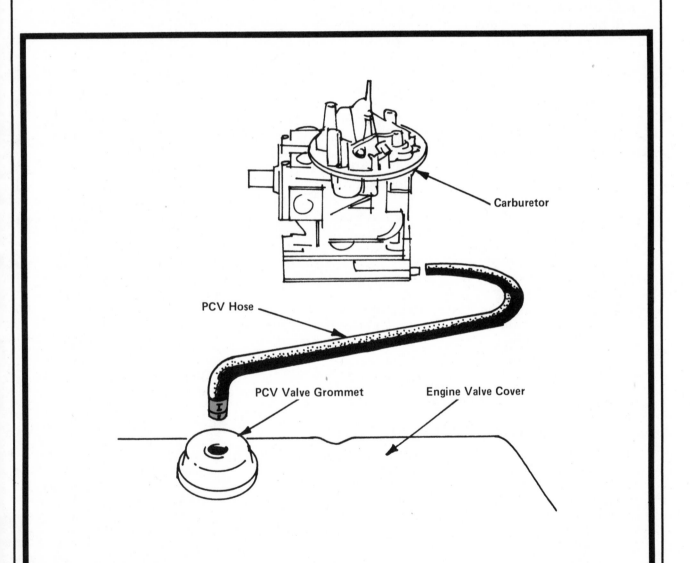

Carburetor

PCV Hose

PCV Valve Grommet

Engine Valve Cover

The PCV valve is located near the carburetor end of the PCV valve hose or at the other end—as in this illustration—where it enters the engine valve cover through a rubber grommet.

the next step is to test the PCV valve. Here is how to do it:

1. Open the hood and remove the air cleaner housing.
2. Look at the area near the base of the carburetor. There will be a hose about ¾ inch in diameter. The PCV valve will be located near the carburetor end of this hose or at the other end entering the engine valve cover through a rubber grommet.
3. Start the engine and let it run at idle speed.
4. Using your hand, pinch the hose connected to the PCV valve. If the valve is operating, you will be able to hear the engine idle speed decline. If the engine idle speed does drop, the PCV system and valve are operating satisfactorily. Stop the engine and reinstall the air cleaner housing.
5. If no decline in engine speed is noted, remove the PCV valve from the engine. Either pull it from the rubber grommet in the engine valve cover by using pliers and wiggling it back and forth, or use pliers to remove it from the vent hose. In some instances, the hoses can be pulled off the valve at both ends. **NOTE:** If the grommet comes out with the PCV valve, it can be difficult to replace it.

Soaking the grommet with motor oil will make it easier to reinstall.

6. Place the PCV valve in a cleaning solution for about 15 minutes. Use a solvent sold for this purpose to clean the PCV valve. **CAUTION:** Don't use gasoline! It is too hazardous.
7. After about 15 minutes, remove the PCV valve from the solvent and allow it to dry.
8. Reinstall the PCV valve and reconnect the hose, using pliers or a screwdriver to secure the hose clamp if necessary. Otherwise, slip the hose over its connections.
9. Start the engine and repeat Step 4.
10. If no decline in engine speed is noted, replace the PCV valve with a new one.

Replacing a PCV Valve. If the PCV valve must be replaced, here is how to do it:

1. Locate the PCV valve.
2. Disconnect the PCV system hose from the PCV valve. This may be done by simply pulling the hose from the valve or by removing a hose clamp with pliers or a screwdriver and then pulling the hose free of the valve.
3. If it is an in-line valve, use pliers to remove it or just pull off the hoses, depending on the hose

connection. If the valve is located in a rubber grommet in the engine valve cover, remove it with pliers. Wiggle it back and forth while pulling it from the grommet. **NOTE:** If the grommet comes out with the PCV valve, it can be difficult to replace it. Soaking the grommet with engine oil will make it easier to reinstall.

4. Purchase the correct PCV valve for your engine.
5. Replace the new PCV valve by reversing Steps 2 and 3.
6. Reinstall the air cleaner housing.

Replacing a PCV Breather Filter Element. On most model cars, there also is a breather filter element for the PCV system. It is located inside the air cleaner housing. If your car is equipped with one, this element also should be replaced periodically. Consult your owner's manual for replacement recommendations. To replace this breather filter element:

1. Remove the air cleaner housing cover.
2. Remove the air filter element.
3. Remove the PCV breather filter retaining clip with pliers.
4. Remove the PCV breather filter.
5. Purchase a new PCV breather filter and install it by reversing Steps 1 through 4.

Servicing the Fuel System

Good carburetion service is mainly directed at the carburetor, but other fuel system components also need inspection and maintenance during a tune-up. The engine's air cleaner, like the carburetor, collects dirt that can hamper its efficient operation. All the mechanical linkage that is part of the carburetor is designed to operate without lubrication, but dirt collects there and must be removed. If these parts are kept clean, the checks and tests that we'll cover will be much easier for you to do.

If you tune your car's engine no more than twice a year, you should always inspect the air cleaner and carburetor for visible dirt. The solvent used to clean carburetors is strong enough to remove paint, so it should be used only on unpainted surfaces. The solvent you use on the air cleaners should be a petroleum-based product such as fuel oil, oleum, or odorless paint thinner.

CAUTION: Never use gasoline or lacquer thinner to clean engine parts. Their fumes are toxic and, more importantly, they are highly flammable. Both gasoline and lacquer thinner have such low flash points that no spark is needed to cause them to burst into flame.

Cleaning the Carburetor. (Phase 1).
For this job, you will need about one cup of carburetor cleaner; a clean, open container such as a soup can; golf tees; a small paintbrush; wrench (optional); and a supply of clean cloths. Follow these steps:

1. Park the car in a well-ventilated area. If possible, work outdoors.
2. Turn the ignition key to the off position and engage the parking brake. Put the transmission in the neutral or park position.
3. Raise the hood, and place a protective covering on both front fenders.
4. Disconnect all hoses leading to the air cleaner housing. Pay attention to their locations. If necessary, make a sketch of the assembly to indicate where each connection is made. This will ease reassembly. Plug vacuum hoses with golf tees to prevent

dirt from entering.

NOTE: on some model cars, the Positive Crankcase Ventilation (PCV) filter hose must also be removed. If so, you will see a pipe or hose coming from an engine valve cover. Usually, there's a small piece of hose at the end of the pipe connecting it to the housing. Actually, the hose connects the PCV filter, which is inside the air cleaner housing. Simply pull the hose away from the air cleaner housing.

5. Remove the carburetor air cleaner housing. Generally, there's a wing nut in the top center of the housing's cover. Sometimes, a regular hex-head nut is used to secure the air cleaner. If so, you'll need a wrench to loosen it. Remove the nut and lift off the housing. Place the entire housing on a workbench or other work area.
6. With the air cleaner housing removed, you'll now have an unobstructed view of the carburetor. Place some cloths around the lower part of the carburetor to soak up any solvent that

The Fuel System

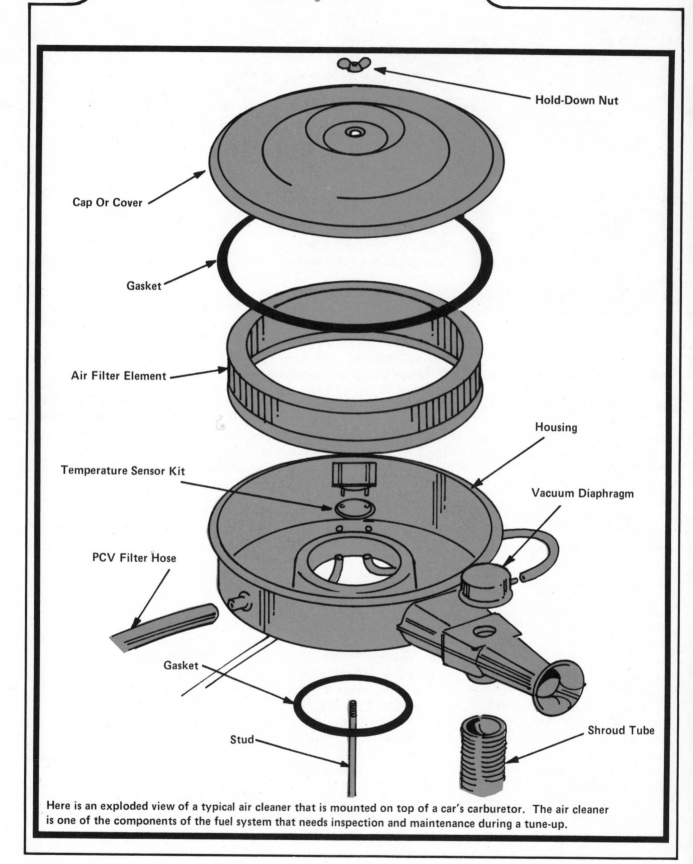

Hold-Down Nut

Cap Or Cover

Gasket

Air Filter Element

Temperature Sensor Kit

PCV Filter Hose

Housing

Vacuum Diaphragm

Gasket

Stud

Shroud Tube

Here is an exploded view of a typical air cleaner that is mounted on top of a car's carburetor. The air cleaner is one of the components of the fuel system that needs inspection and maintenance during a tune-up.

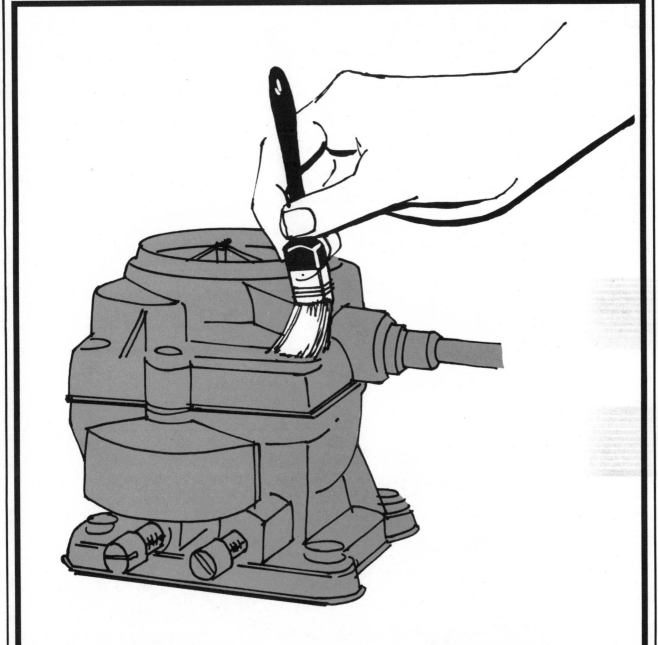

After placing some cloths around the lower part of the carburetor to catch any solvent that drips, use a paintbrush to apply carburetor cleaner to the carburetor. Don't force the brush down inside the carburetor.

will drip during cleaning.

7. Pour about one cup of carburetor cleaner into a clean metal container.

Hold the can of cleaner in one hand, close to the carburetor, so the solvent will not spill on painted

surfaces and damage them.

8. Brush the cleaner on the inside of the open

carburetor throat. Use the cleaner sparingly, but thoroughly brush each area that can be easily reached. Don't, however, force the brush down inside the carburetor. Brush the tarnished parts

9. Brush the cleaner on all the outside parts of the carburetor. The purpose here, however, is not to clean, but simply to wet the exterior parts. Use a minimum amount of brushing. Allow at least 10 minutes for the cleaner to soak into the accumulated dirt.

While you are waiting for the carburetor cleaner to work, you can save some time by cleaning the air cleaner housing.

Cleaning the Air Cleaner. Cleaning the air cleaner housing takes only about 10 minutes and it can possibly reduce your car's fuel consumption. For this cleaning job, you will need about one cup of the petroleum-based solvent; a clean, open metal container such as a coffee can; a small paintbrush, and a supply of clean cloths.

1. Remove the housing cover of the air cleaner and the filter element.
2. Pour about one cup of petroleum solvent into the clean metal can.
3. Dampen a cloth with solvent and wipe as much of the inside surface of the housing as you can reach.
4. Using a paintbrush, apply solvent to any inside surface that you can't reach with the cloth.
5. Apply the solvent to the outside surfaces of the housing.
6. Wipe the entire air

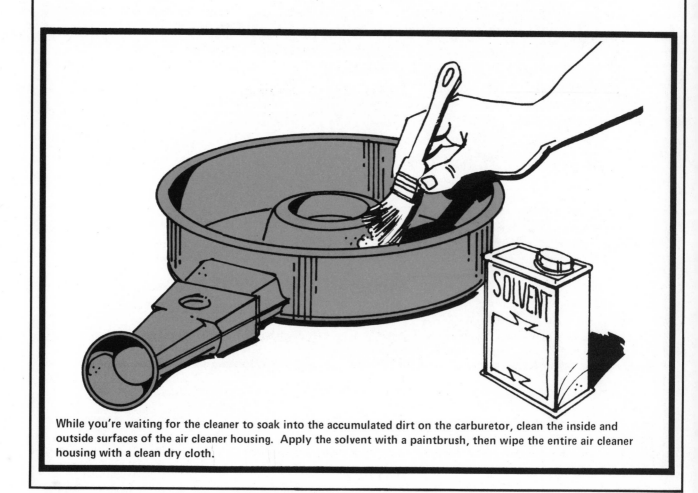

While you're waiting for the cleaner to soak into the accumulated dirt on the carburetor, clean the inside and outside surfaces of the air cleaner housing. Apply the solvent with a paintbrush, then wipe the entire air cleaner housing with a clean dry cloth.

cleaner housing with a clean dry cloth. Wipe the linkage to eliminate any solvent that could drip off the housing after it has been replaced on the carburetor.

7. Use a clean dry cloth to buff the housing's exterior surfaces until they are clean and bright.

Replacing the Air Cleaner Filter Element. Air cleaner filter service consists of replacing or cleaning the filter element and checking the operation of thermostatically controlled parts on the air cleaner. A dirty filter restricts air flow to the engine and increases fuel consumption. It's good practice to check the filter at least every 3,000 to 4,000 miles of driving and replace it when necessary. Your car may have one of several types of filters. Be sure you obtain a correct replacement for your car.

CLEANERS WITH A PAPER ELEMENT. Since the air cleaner has already been removed from the engine, inspect the element for dirt and for torn or broken filter paper. You can test the air filter to see if it needs replacement by holding a bright light (a 100-watt light bulb on an extension cord will do) on the inside of the air filter. Look at the outside of the air filter as you pass it over the light. If light does not show through the air filter paper, replace the air filter with a new one. Don't blow air through the air filter from the inside. This could damage the air filter, and if you put a damaged air filter back in the housing, it would just allow more dirt to reach the engine.

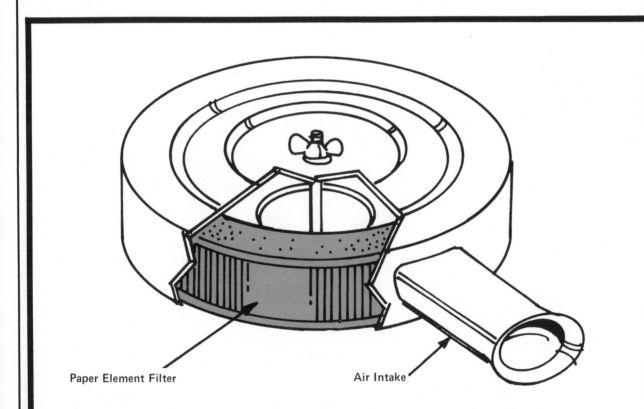

Paper Element Filter   Air Intake

If your air cleaner uses a paper filter element, you can see if it needs replacing by holding a bright light on the inside of the filter. If light doesn't show through the paper, replace the filter with a new one.

Filter elements should be replaced at the car maker's recommended intervals or more often if dirty or damaged. **NOTE:** Oil on the filter element may indicate a fault in the engine's PCV system.

CLEANERS WITH A POLYURETHANE ELEMENT. A polyurethane filter element is serviced by removing the polyurethane wrapper from its metal support screen and washing it in a petroleum-based solvent. Carefully squeeze excess solvent from the wrapper and then dip it in clean SAE 10 W 30 motor oil. Carefully squeeze out the excess oil. Then, replace the polyurethane wrapper on the screen. It will fit loosely at first but will tighten as it dries. If torn, the wrapper must be replaced.

OTHER TYPES OF AIR CLEANERS. Some older cars and trucks use an oil-soaked foam air filter. This filtering element should periodically be cleaned (at least at each tune-up) with solvent and dried. Then, the element should be re-oiled by lightly coating it with motor oil (not too much) before reinstalling it in its housing. Your owner's manual should provide more detail.

There also is another type of air filter called an oil bath filter. This type uses the lower portion of the air filter housing as an oil bath. The filter element, usually a wire mesh of some sort, sits partially in the oil. Air entering the housing passes through the mesh, through the oil and into the engine.

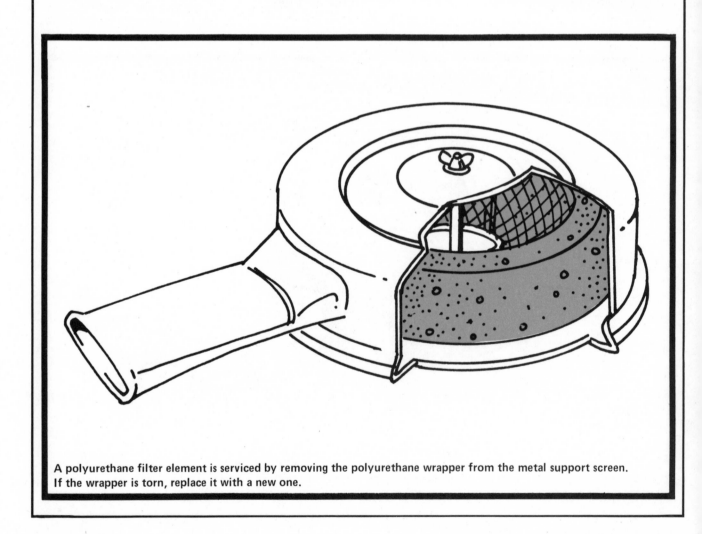

A polyurethane filter element is serviced by removing the polyurethane wrapper from the metal support screen. If the wrapper is torn, replace it with a new one.

To clean a polyurethane filter element, wash it in petroleum-based solvent and carefully squeeze the excess solvent from the wrapper. Then dip the wrapper in clean SAE 10 W 30 motor oil. Carefully squeeze out the excess oil and replace the wrapper on its support screen.

The dirty oil in such an air filter must be replaced on a regular basis according to the car maker's recommendations. Here is how to do it:

1. Remove the air cleaner housing cover by loosening the nut in the center of the cover.
2. Remove the wire mesh filter element.
3. Remove the filter housing from the carburetor by lifting it off.
4. Clean the wire mesh filter element with solvent and let it air dry.
5. Empty the oil from the cleaner housing and clean out any sediment that may be present in the bottom of the housing. Do this by washing the unit with a petroleum-based solvent (never gasoline!) and wiping it with a clean cloth.
6. Replace the housing on the carburetor.
7. Put clean engine oil in the housing up to the marked level.
8. Reinstall the wire mesh filter element.
9. Reinstall the housing cover and tighten the nut.

Cleaning the Carburetor (Phase 2).
Once you've cleaned the air cleaner housing, and cleaned or replaced the air filter element, set the housing aside and resume cleaning the carburetor.

1. After about 10 minutes, apply additional cleaner with the brush, starting at the top of the carburetor. The dirt will now come away and be carried down the sides of the carburetor to be soaked up by the cloths. Continue applying cleaner until all of the carburetor's exterior is clean and bright.
2. Remove the cloths placed around the carburetor and dispose of them and the used cleaner properly.
3. Make sure that there are no pools of liquid cleaner remaining on the lower recesses of the carburetor and its mounting area. If there are, wipe them dry with a cloth. Use a dry cloth wrapped around a screwdriver blade to blot up any wet areas that cannot be reached by hand.

CAUTION: The next step is to start the engine without the air cleaner housing attached. There is a possibility, however, that the engine will backfire through the carburetor. *Do not* allow anyone to peer into the engine compartment while the engine is being started. This type of backfire can cause a vapor (air) fire that is harmless to the engine, but can seriously burn someone too close to the area.

4. Attempt to start the car. If the engine starts immediately, turn the ignition to the off position. If the engine refuses to start immediately, continue cranking the engine for about 5 seconds. Then, turn the ignition key to the off position. This action will draw any cleaner into the carburetor intake manifold, rendering it harmless.
5. Install the cleaned air cleaner housing, securing all hose and pipe connections to the housing. Be sure that no wires or hoses are caught between the cover and the housing. **NOTE:** Never overtighten an air cleaner wing nut or clamp on the carburetor. Overtightening may distort the carburetor air horn and cause faulty automatic choke operation.
6. Start the engine and allow it to idle for about 2 minutes.
7. Turn the ignition key to the off position.

Checking the Air Cleaner's Automatic Temperature Control. A few simple checks can determine whether the air cleaner's automatic temperature control is working correctly. When the engine is off, the vacuum motor spring in a vacuum-operated air cleaner should move the damper to close the hot-air passage and open the cold-air passage through the snorkel. If this

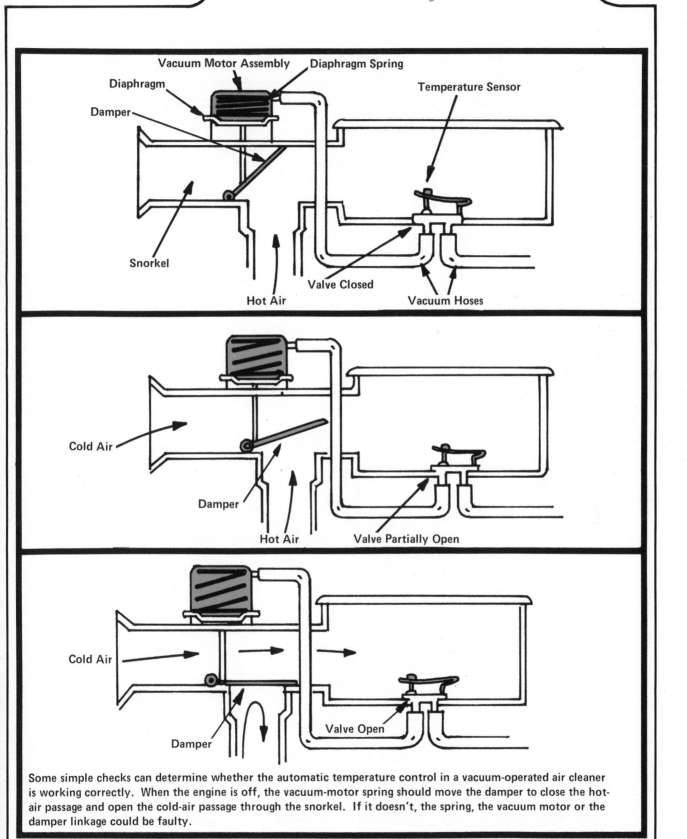

Some simple checks can determine whether the automatic temperature control in a vacuum-operated air cleaner is working correctly. When the engine is off, the vacuum-motor spring should move the damper to close the hot-air passage and open the cold-air passage through the snorkel. If it doesn't, the spring, the vacuum motor or the damper linkage could be faulty.

is not the case, the spring, the vacuum motor or the damper linkage is faulty.

Check the vacuum motor by applying vacuum directly from the intake manifold to the vacuum motor. You can do this by disconnecting the two vacuum hoses leading to the temperature sensor and connecting them together with a short piece of tubing. The damper should close the cold-air passage in the snorkel. If the damper does not move, check the linkage for binding. When you are satisifed that the vacuum motor and damper are working correctly, you can check the thermostatic sensor:

1. Remove the air cleaner hold-down nut and the housing cover only.

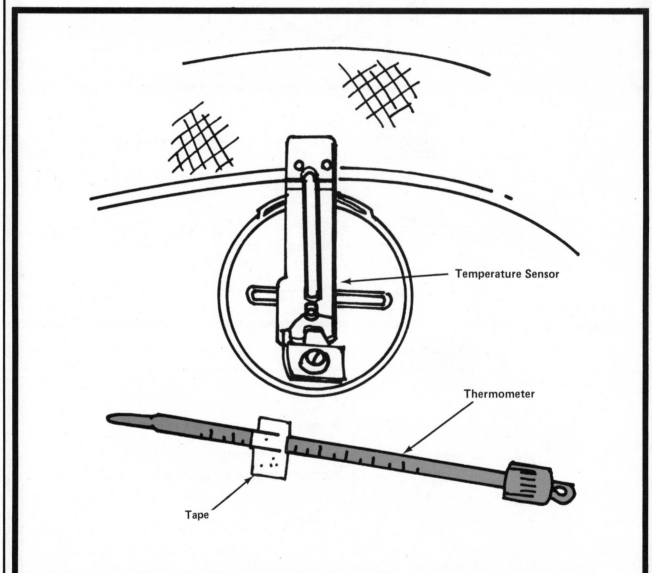

Temperature Sensor

Thermometer

Tape

To check the air cleaner's thermostatic sensor, an ordinary household thermometer can be taped close to the sensor to see whether the damper functions at the proper temperatures.

2. With the engine cold, tape an ordinary household thermometer close to the temperature sensor in the air cleaner housing.
3. Replace the air cleaner cover over the housing but don't secure it with the hold-down nut.
4. Start and idle the engine. Then, check to see that vacuum moves the damper to the full hot-air position.
5. When the damper begins to open, lift the air cleaner cover and check the temperature indicated on the thermometer. A temperature of 100° to 110° F. is acceptable. This is the point at which the sensor starts to bleed vacuum from the vacuum motor.
6. When the damper moves to the full cold-air position, check the temperature again. It should be between 130° and 135° F. The sensor should be replaced with a new one if the temperature exceeds 135° F.

NOTE: On engines with a dual-snorkel air cleaner, the damper in the second snorkel is held in the full hot-air position by intake vacuum until the throttle is opened wide. A thermostatic sensor is not used. The drop in vacuum causes the vacuum motor spring to force the damper to the full cold-air position. While the engine is running, you can check the damper operation of such an air cleaner by pulling the throttle wide open from idle. The damper should move to the full cold-air position.

Replacing the Fuel Filter. To run properly, a car's engine must have an adequate supply of fuel at all times. And, the fuel must be as clean as possible. As it passes through the fuel system, fuel is regulated by small orifices or jets. If dirt or any other foreign particles are present, the system could clog up, causing engine performance to suffer.

To prevent this possibility, car makers install fuel filters in the system. To keep the fuel system clean, these filters must be replaced according to the manufacturer's recommendations, or more often if engine performance declines. A dirty fuel filter can cause an engine to act sluggish during acceleration or operation at high speeds. It also can be so clogged with contaminants that the engine will not operate.

Throughout the years, car makers have used several types of fuel filters. The most common one consisted of a porous, ceramic-like element enclosed in a glass housing. Fuel entered the glass housing from the top and was filtered as it passed through the element and into the carburetor. Servicing was performed by removing the glass housing when it looked dirty and by cleaning or replacing the filtering element.

Today, however, all car makers use some form of in-line fuel filter. The filter element is either enclosed in a housing and is replaceable, or the entire unit—housing and element—is replaced. Most filters have rubber hoses secured to their inlet and outlet nipples by small clamps.

While some older General Motors cars had a fuel filter at the end of the fuel line in the fuel tank, most filters are now located on the engine somewhere between the fuel pump and the carburetor. General Motors incorporates an internal fuel filter, mounted in the fuel bowl behind the fuel inlet nut. Ford Motor Company cars have fuel filters that are screwed directly into the carburetor. Chrysler Corporation and American Motors cars have an in-line fuel filter located in the fuel line between the fuel pump and the carburetor. Since there are differences in the replacement of fuel filters depending on the type of car you have, manufacturers' models will be treated separately.

On all cars, however, begin by opening the hood and removing the air cleaner housing. **CAUTION:** A potential fire hazard exists whenever fuel lines are disconnected. Avoid open flames and working in confined areas without ventilation. Depending on the type of fuel filter you have, you'll need the following: replacement fuel filter, clean cloths, pliers or screwdriver, and open-end wrench and flare-nut or tubing wrench.

FORD FILTER REPLACEMENT. Ford Motor Company generally uses a filter that is screwed directly into the carburetor at the end of the fuel line. Gasoline enters the filter housing from the fuel line (or pipe) that comes from the fuel pump. Usually, there is a short piece of rubber hose on the end of the fuel line that connects the fuel line to the fuel filter. In addition, hose clamps usually secure the hose at either end. To replace this filter:

1. Obtain the proper fuel filter replacement before removing the old one.
2. Locate the fuel filter. It is a round, can-like unit that is about 1 inch in diameter.
3. Place a clean cloth between the fuel filter connecting hose and the intake manifold. This will help prevent a potential fire hazard by absorbing any gasoline loss during the removal of the fuel filter. Disconnect the fuel line hose from the end of the fuel filter by removing the hose clamp. Use pliers or a screwdriver, depending on the type of

clamp. After the clamp is removed, pull the hose free of the filter.
4. Remove the fuel filter from the carburetor. This is accomplished by unscrewing the filter counterclockwise. You may have to use a wrench on the end of the filter to turn it. Discard the entire fuel filter.
5. Install the new fuel filter. This is done by screwing the filter clockwise into the carburetor by hand.

Use a wrench only to tighten the filter slightly.
6. Reinstall the fuel line hose located on the end of the fuel line by pushing it onto the end of the fuel filter. Tighten the clamp. Remove any gasoline that may have spilled onto the intake manifold with the cloth and then discard the cloth in a safe manner.
7. Start the engine and check for fuel leaks. Repair any leaks by

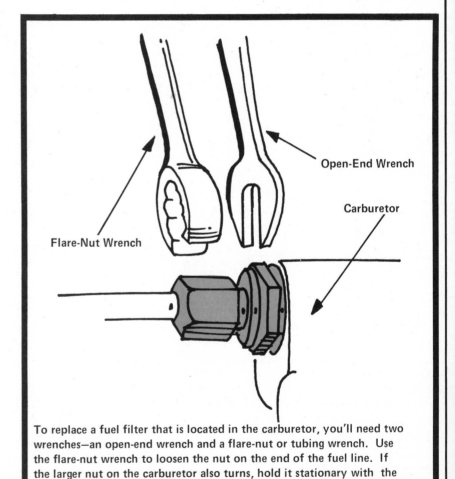

To replace a fuel filter that is located in the carburetor, you'll need two wrenches—an open-end wrench and a flare-nut or tubing wrench. Use the flare-nut wrench to loosen the nut on the end of the fuel line. If the larger nut on the carburetor also turns, hold it stationary with the open-end wrench.

tightening the filter or hose clamp as necessary.
8. Reinstall the air cleaner housing.

GENERAL MOTORS FILTER REPLACEMENT. Most General Motors cars have the fuel filter housed right in the carburetor where the fuel line from the fuel pump is connected. Generally, the fuel filter element is made of bronze or paper. In this case, only the element itself is

replaced. Be sure to obtain the correct replacement element before removing the old element. To replace this fuel filter:

1. Locate the fuel line (pipe) that comes from the fuel pump to the carburetor.
2. Place a clean cloth between the fuel inlet nut at the carburetor and the intake manifold. This will help absorb any gasoline loss during removal of the filter. Disconnect the

fuel line at the carburetor. You will need two wrenches for this, about a 1 inch open-end wrench and a flare-nut or tubing wrench, usually $\frac{9}{16}$ or $\frac{5}{8}$ inch in size. Using the flare-nut wrench, loosen the nut on the end of the fuel line. If the larger nut on the carburetor also turns, hold it stationary with the open-end wrench. This will be necessary to prevent damage to the

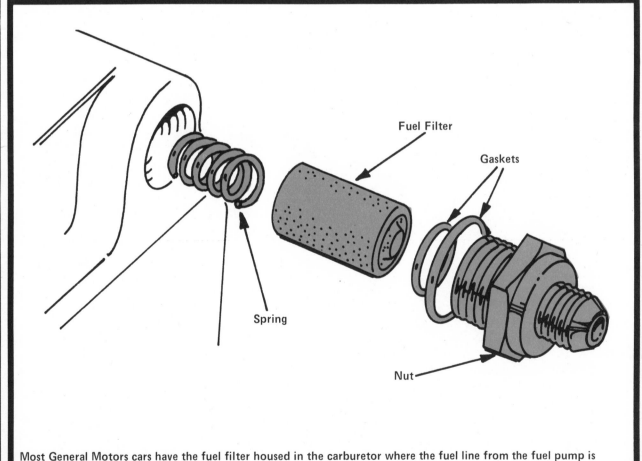

Most General Motors cars have the fuel filter housed in the carburetor where the fuel line from the fuel pump is connected. Only the filter element, generally made of bronze or paper, need be replaced.

fuel line when disconnecting it.

3. With the fuel line disconnected, loosen the larger nut on the carburetor with the larger wrench. This one holds the fuel filter. There is a light spring inside the filter element housing that could pop out if you are not careful, so remove this nut slowly. Also, notice the direction the old fuel filter is facing as you remove it. It usually is marked in some way as to the direction of fuel flow. If it's installed backwards, fuel flow will be restricted.

4. Install the new fuel filter in the carburetor—don't forget the spring—and with a wrench tighten the nut that holds it in the housing.

5. Reconnect the fuel line to the carburetor and tighten the nut with the flare-nut wrench. Remove the cloth and any gasoline that may have spilled on the intake manifold during the removal and installation of the filter.

6. Start the engine and check for fuel leaks. Repair them if necessary by tightening the nuts on the fuel line and carburetor.

7. Reinstall the air cleaner housing.

CHRYSLER, AMC FILTER REPLACEMENT. Chrysler and AMC generally use an in-line fuel filter. This is a canister-type filter that is completely discarded. There will be rubber hoses on both ends of the filter, so you will have hose clamps, either spring-type or screw-type, to loosen. To replace these fuel filters:

1. Locate the filter. It will be in the fuel line (pipe) that leads to the carburetor from the fuel pump.

2. Loosen the hose clamps on either end of the fuel filter, using a pliers or screwdriver, depending on the type of clamp.

3. Remove the fuel filter by pulling back the rubber hose on either end of the filter housing. Note the direction of fuel flow as marked on the filter.

4. Inspect the rubber hoses for signs of fuel leakage, cracking or other deterioration of the hoses. Replace as necessary, obtaining the correct hose from your auto supply store.

5. Install the new fuel filter. Note the direction of fuel flow marked on the filter housing. Install it in the correct position. Place the hoses over the filter housing inlet and outlet. Tighten the hose clamps just enough to prevent fuel leakage.

6. Start the engine and check for fuel leaks. Repair them if necessary by tightening the hose clamps.

7. Reinstall the air cleaner housing.

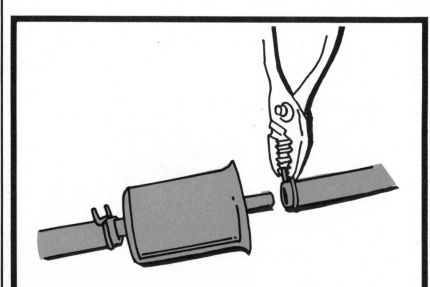

Chrysler and AMC cars generally use an in-line type of fuel filter. Loosen the hose clamps on either end with pliers or screwdriver, depending on the type of clamp used. When installing a new filter, note the direction of fuel flow marked on the filter so that it is installed in the correct position.

Servicing the Ignition System

The ignition system, one of several electrical systems in your car, is mainly designed to ignite the air/fuel mixture that is drawn into the engine through the carburetor. This system is separated into two circuits: the primary or low-voltage circuit and the secondary or high-voltage circuit. However, they function together and are interdependent.

The primary circuit consists of the battery, ignition switch, the primary part of the ignition coil (it has a dual function), the primary side of the distributor (it, too, has a dual function), and, finally, the wires connecting each of these components to complete the electrical circuitry.

Components of the secondary circuit include the secondary part of the ignition coil, the secondary side of the distributor, and, finally, the spark plugs.

After you've inspected, cleaned, and tested the battery, the main components left to be serviced in a basic tune-up are the spark plugs and the distributor. If, however, your car has a breakerless electronic ignition as most new models do, consult your car's service manual to determine what maintenance is required. Servicing electronic ignitions generally requires special equipment and should be left to a qualified mechanic. So, once the spark plugs have been replaced, you can proceed to the section on electronic ignition timing.

Removing the Spark Plugs. For this step in the tune-up operation, you'll need the following tools and materials: extension work light; masking tape and pencil to label spark plug cables; spark plug boot puller (optional); spark plug socket, extension, and ratchet wrench; clean cloths, and solvent.

To remove spark plugs, follow this general procedure:

1. If the engine is hot, allow it and the exhaust manifold to cool sufficiently so that you don't burn yourself.
2. Carefully remove the spark plug wires or cables by grasping each one by the plug boot or hooded cap shield and twisting gently while pulling. Don't jerk on the cable or you may damage the delicate end. You also could purchase a spark plug boot puller tool to ease this task.
3. Make careful note of where each spark plug cable goes. On some cars, the cable lengths may be similar. To make sure you will replace them properly later, label them before removal with pieces of masking tape. Wipe the cables clean.
4. Loosen each spark plug *only* one or two turns, turning counterclockwise with a ratchet wrench and spark plug socket of the proper size.
5. Using a cloth dampened with solvent, wipe any dirt from around the base of each spark plug. It's best to put on a pair of safety goggles and blow the dirt away with compressed air to keep it from falling into the cylinders when the plugs are completely removed. But since this isn't usually feasible, an alternate method is to turn on the car's ignition switch to crank the engine for a few seconds

The Ignition System

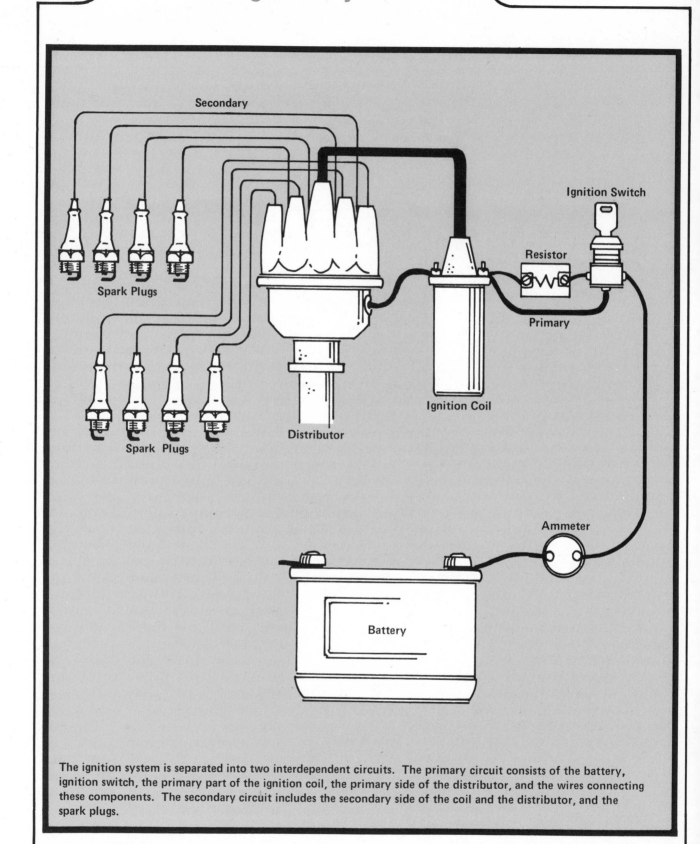

Secondary

Spark Plugs

Spark Plugs

Distributor

Ignition Coil

Resistor

Primary

Ignition Switch

Ammeter

Battery

The ignition system is separated into two interdependent circuits. The primary circuit consists of the battery, ignition switch, the primary part of the ignition coil, the primary side of the distributor, and the wires connecting these components. The secondary circuit includes the secondary side of the coil and the distributor, and the spark plugs.

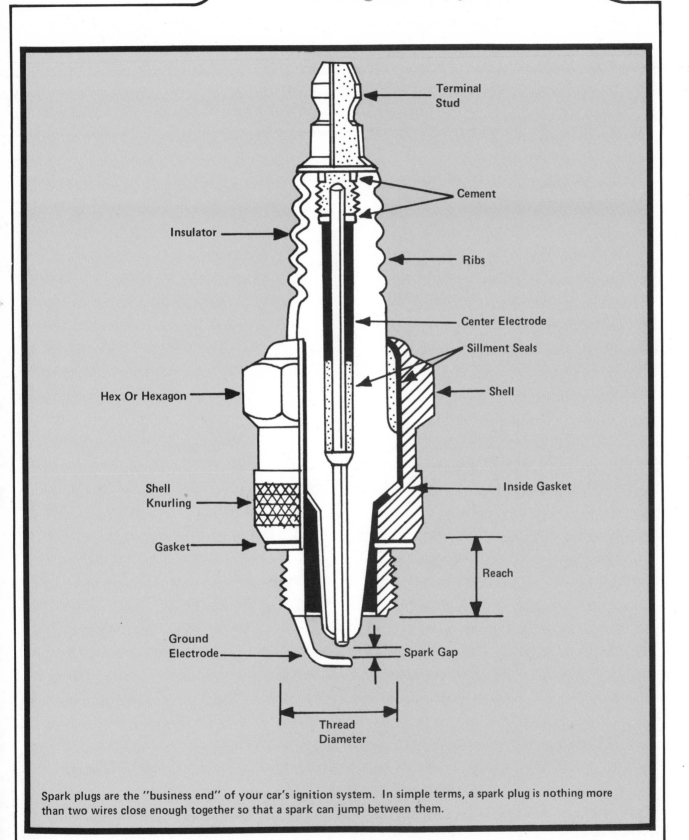

Spark plugs are the "business end" of your car's ignition system. In simple terms, a spark plug is nothing more than two wires close enough together so that a spark can jump between them.

so that any loose dirt around the spark plugs will be blown away.

6. Remove the spark plugs one at a time and arrange each one in a tray or on your workbench by cylinder number or in the order of removal for inspection. **NOTE:** On gasketed plugs, be sure the metal gasket is removed with the plug. Chrysler Sixes and hemispherical V8 engines use gasket-type plugs installed in tubes without gaskets.

Diagnosing the Spark Plugs. An experienced mechanic can tell a lot about the condition of a car's engine by examining its spark plugs. You can too. In fact, the ability to examine a plug's electrodes and insulator tip to determine the plug's operating condition is an important part of spark plug service. To help you do a good job of spark plug

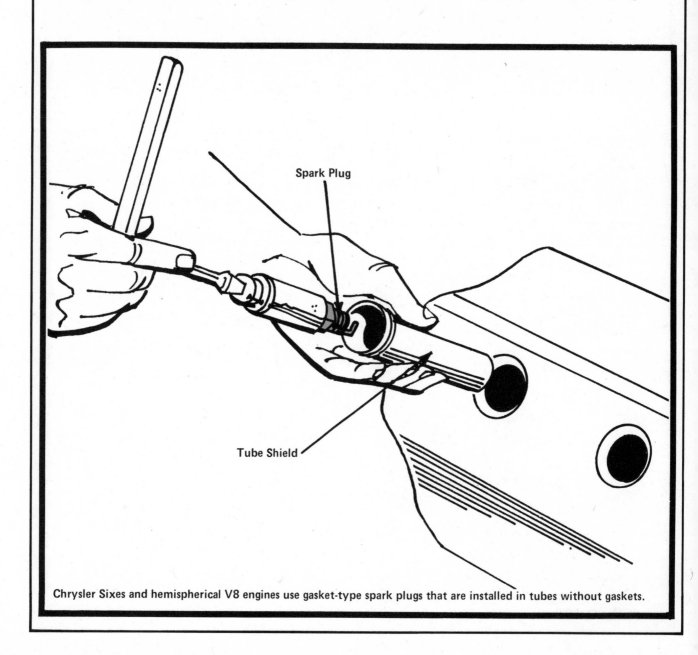

Spark Plug

Tube Shield

Chrysler Sixes and hemispherical V8 engines use gasket-type spark plugs that are installed in tubes without gaskets.

inspection, study the following examples of spark plugs operating under various conditions:

NORMAL PLUG. This is what you would always like to see—a light brown or gray-tan color on the insulator tip and clean electrodes with only slight wear. There is a minimal amount of erosion at the center electrode. You can conclude that the plug is operating at the correct temperatures and the car's engine is sound. Conclusion: Such plugs can be cleaned and regapped.

OVERHEATED PLUG. On such plugs, both electrodes are eroded and the insulator tip is white and free of deposits. The insulator tip may also be blistered or cracked. This condition is due to the heat range of the plug being too hot for the engine's operating conditions. Contributing factors may be over-advanced engine timing, a heat riser valve that is stuck in the closed position or an air/fuel mixture that is too lean. Conclusion: It's a good practice to replace such plugs once the basic cause has been determined and corrected.

CARBON-FOULED PLUG. Soft, dry, sooty deposits on the plug's electrodes, insulator tip, and inside the shell generally indicate that the plug temperature is too low for the engine's

Normal Spark Plug

Overheated Spark Plug

Carbon-Fouled Spark Plug

Oil-Fouled Spark Plug

operating conditions. Possible causes include an over-rich air/fuel mixture, retarded engine timing, a sticking choke, a heat riser valve that is stuck open, low engine temperatures, and excessive idling and low-speed driving. If a spark plug appears to have been operating too hot or too cold, don't overlook the possibility that plugs with the wrong heat range were installed in the engine. Conclusion: After the problem has been determined and corrected, such plugs can be cleaned and regapped.

OIL-FOULED PLUG. Dark, wet deposits on the electrodes, insulator tip, and shell indicate that oil is getting into the combustion chamber somehow. Oil fouling may be caused by several kinds of engine wear, including old age. Conclusion: The use of spark plugs that are one or two heat ranges hotter than specified for the engine should reduce oil fouling but it's only a temporary solution. Sooner or later, the basic problem will have to be corrected. Oil-fouled plugs can be cleaned and regapped.

DETONATION. Detonation, generally referred to as "knocking" or "pinging," occurs when over-advanced ignition timing or low-octane fuel causes combustion conditions that result in severe mechanical shock. These explosive, hammer-like blows can damage a piston or the spark plug, and may eventually fracture the plug's electrode. Conclusion: The cause of the problem must be corrected, and the damaged plug should be replaced.

TURBULENCE-BURNED PLUG. The shape of the combustion chambers in some engines causes hot gases to always flow over the tips of plugs in the same direction at a high velocity. Conclusion: Such plugs have to be inspected and replaced more often.

SPLASH-FOULED PLUG. This condition is caused by deposits in the combustion chamber suddenly breaking loose from pistons and valves and "splashing" against a hot plug insulator. It can occur after a long-delayed tune-up. Conclusion: Too much splash fouling can short out the plug. Before this occurs, the plugs should be cleaned and regapped.

CORE- OR GAP-BRIDGED PLUG. Core- or gap-bridging is usually due to the same conditions as splash fouling. The difference is mainly in degree. Excessive deposits can form a bridge between the plug's insulator and the shell, producing a short. This is most common in engines where oil control is poor or in engines which are used in slow-speed, start-

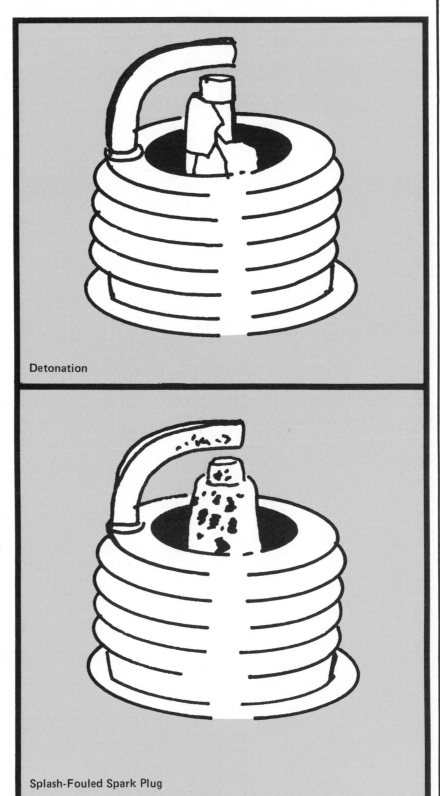

Detonation

Splash-Fouled Spark Plug

Ash-Fouled Spark Plug

Insulator Glazing On Spark Plug

and-stop service. This splashing can also bridge the gap across the electrodes to short out the plug. Conclusion: Sometimes the plug can be cleaned and regapped.

INSULATOR-CHIPPED PLUG. A cracked or broken insulator usually results from bending the center electrode to set the correct spark gap. To avoid such damage, bend only the side electrode when gapping a spark plug. Under certain conditions, a chipped insulator can result from severe detonations. Conclusion: Such plugs must be replaced.

ASH-FOULED PLUG. If there are excessive deposits of light brown or white ash on the ground and center electrodes, the cause may be the type of fuel or oil being used. Conclusion: In this case, you can clean or replace the plug and first try changing the brand of gasoline to see if that solves the problem. If it doesn't, you know you are faced with at least an oil and filter change with a different brand of oil and, most likely, some engine work.

INSULATOR GLAZING ON PLUG. On such plugs, normal combustion deposits on the firing tip do not have an opportunity to burn off. Instead, they melt to form a conductive coating. Conclusion: Generally, glazing cannot be removed by normal cleaning procedures and it is better to replace the plugs. If the condition persists, you may have to use a plug that is one step colder to solve the problem.

PREIGNITION. This is just what it implies—ignition of the fuel charge prior to the timed spark. It can be caused by combustion chamber deposits that become incandescent; hot spots in the combustion chamber due to poor control of engine heat; piston scuffing, caused by inadequate lubrication or improper clearance of engine parts; detonation; cross-firing; or a spark plug heat range that is too high for the engine. Often, preignition can damage the piston head. Conclusion: The cause must be determined and corrected. Damaged plugs must be replaced.

WORN-OUT PLUG. Worn center and ground electrodes indicate that a plug has given its full service life and should be replaced. A brownish-gray color on the insulator tip shows that the plug's heat range is correct. Conclusion: Since the ground electrode cannot be squared with the center electrode, such plugs should be replaced.

Cleaning the Spark Plugs. After examining the spark plugs, you'll have to decide whether to clean and regap

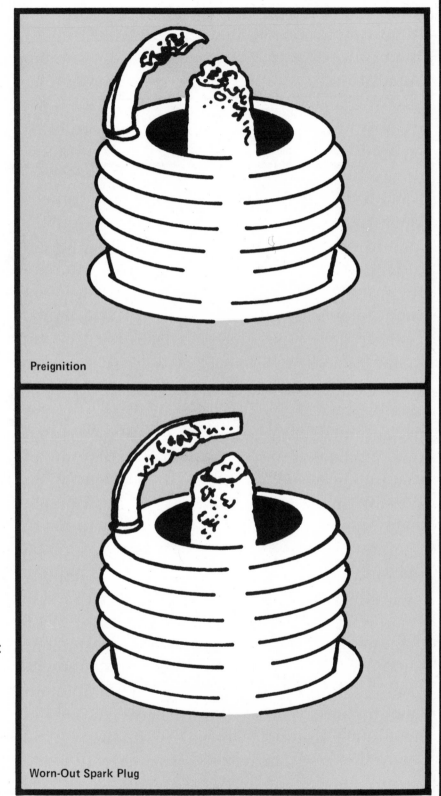

Preignition

Worn-Out Spark Plug

them or install a new set. Often, it's easier to install new spark plugs than to clean and regap old ones, especially if they are near the end of their service life of 10,000 to 12,000 miles.

However, used plugs that are not damaged or excessively worn can be cleaned. For this, you'll need the following tools and materials: clean cloths, solvent, safety goggles, wire brush, and an ignition point file.

Follow this procedure:

1. Using a clean cloth, wipe oil and grease from the outside of the plugs. If

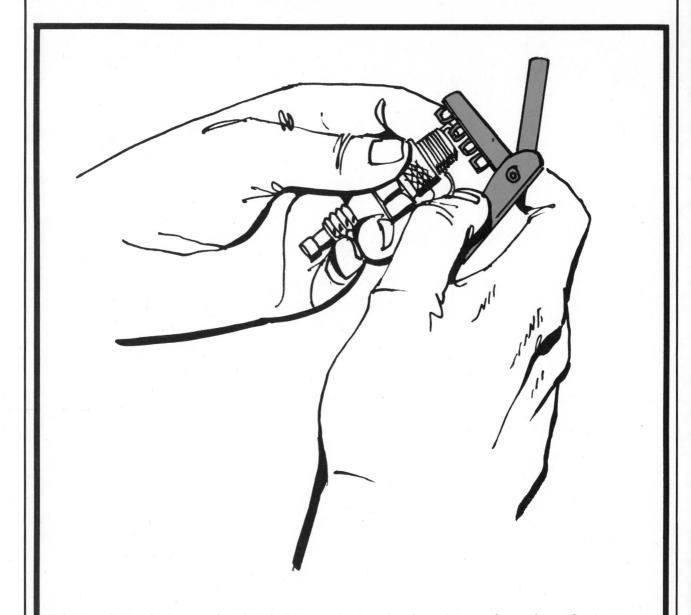

Before installation, both new and used spark plugs must be gapped to the engine manufacturer's specifications. Gapping data can be found in your vehicle owner's manual.

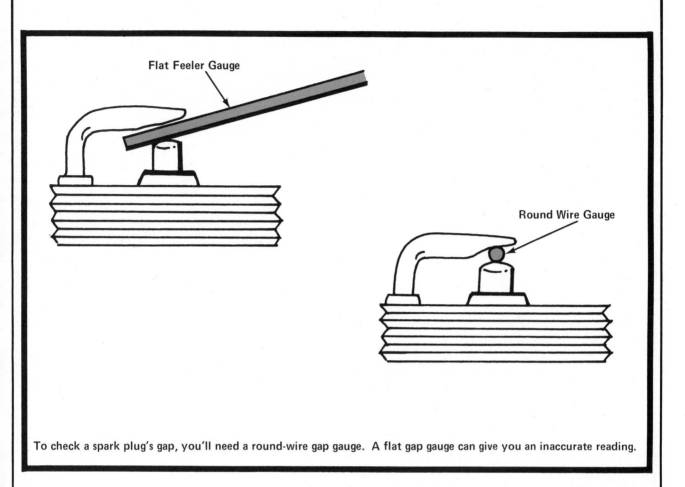

Flat Feeler Gauge

Round Wire Gauge

To check a spark plug's gap, you'll need a round-wire gap gauge. A flat gap gauge can give you an inaccurate reading.

necessary, use a small amount of solvent. Dry the plugs thoroughly with a clean cloth.

2. Put on a pair of safety goggles and use a hand-held wire brush to clean the threads and electrode ends of the plugs.

3. File the center electrode of each plug until it is clean and flat. File the inside surface of the ground electrode of each plug until the surface appears shiny.

Gapping the Spark Plugs. Before installation later in

the tune-up, both new and used spark plugs must be gapped to the engine manufacturer's specifications. This information can be found in your vehicle owner's manual. Although new plugs may be pregapped by the manufacturer, don't assume that they are gapped correctly. In addition, spark plugs used with many electronic ignition systems require wide gaps in the 0.060- to 0.080-inch range. Plug manufacturers supply special plugs for wide-gap applications. Wide-gap and

narrow-gap plugs are made in identical heat ranges, the only difference is in the preset gap. **CAUTION:** Don't attempt to set a narrow-gap plug to wide-gap specifications, or vice versa. Electrode damage will result.

To check a spark plug's gap, you'll need a round-wire gap gauge. A flat gap gauge is likely to give you an inaccurate reading. To change the gap, use the plug-gapping tool. Carefully bend the side—and only this electrode—to the required gap.

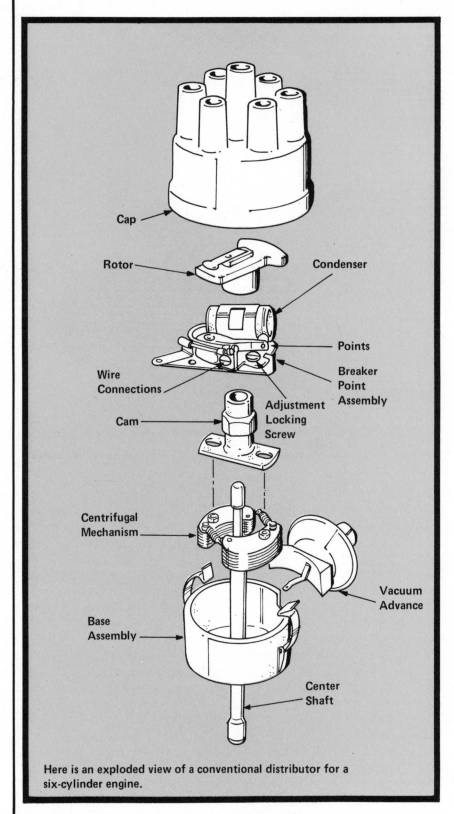

Cap

Rotor

Condenser

Points

Wire Connections

Breaker Point Assembly

Cam

Adjustment Locking Screw

Centrifugal Mechanism

Vacuum Advance

Base Assembly

Center Shaft

Here is an exploded view of a conventional distributor for a six-cylinder engine.

Servicing the Distributor. Your car's distributor—the heart of the ignition system—requires periodic inspection, cleaning, and adjustment, as well as replacement of some components to keep it in proper working order unless it happens to be a breakerless electronic ignition. The breakerless system replaces the mechanical breaker-point distributor system with an electronic one. We'll discuss electronic ignitions after covering the breaker-point system. If your car has an electronic ignition, there's no need to check point gap or dwell so you can proceed to the section on "Installing the Spark Plugs" and then to the section on timing electronic ignitions.

The breaker-point distributor, meanwhile, can be checked and serviced without removing it from the engine. On some vehicles, however, it may be necessary to remove the air cleaner housing to make the distributor accessible.

For this stage of the tune-up, you'll need the following tools and materials: small screwdrivers, a set of open-end ignition wrenches, replacement points and condenser for your distributor, clean cloths, solvent, cam lubricant, flat steel feeler gauge, dwell tachometer (optional), jumper wire (optional), golf tees, remote starter switch (optional), and hexagonal Allen wrench (optional).

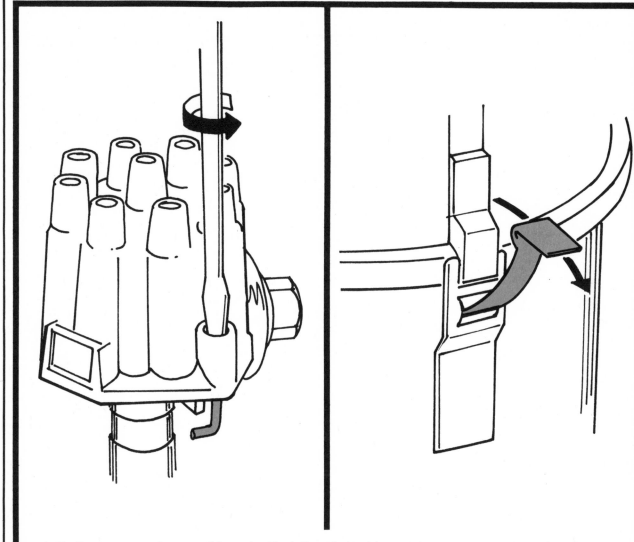

A distributor cap may be secured by spring-like bails or L-shaped screw clamps located on opposite sides of the distributor.

THE DISTRIBUTOR CAP. On most engines, there should be sufficient slack in the cables leading to the distributor so that it isn't necessary to remove them. Follow these steps:

1. Remove the distributor cap. It may be secured by L-shaped screw clamps or spring-like bails located on opposite sides of the distributor. Simply flip open the bails. If, however, the cap is held by screw clamps, turn each clamp hold-down one-half turn clockwise or counterclockwise while pushing down on a screwdriver to release the cap. Lift off the cap and clean it with a dry cloth inside and outside.

2. Look inside the cap. You will find metal spikes under each wire connection (the spikes are inside the cap, the

connections on the outside). There also will be a black "button" made of carbon under the center tower. This is where the rotor connects with the cap.

3. Look for signs of burned or corroded metal spikes, a deteriorated carbon button, corrosion inside the cap towers or any other signs of cracks or damage to the inside of the cap.

4. Inspect the outside of the cap. Look for cracks or signs of other damage to the cap. Also, carefully inspect for cracks around the wire tower connections.

5. Inspect both the inside and outside of the distributor cap for signs of carbon tracks. These will appear as black lines running from a wire connection tower or metal spike.

6. If you find any of the conditions described, the distributor cap will have to be replaced.

DISTRIBUTOR ROTOR. You'll find the distributor rotor on top of the distributor's center shaft. The rotor may be a large, flat object secured to the shaft by two screws. It can be removed with a screwdriver. Most, however, will be the smaller type

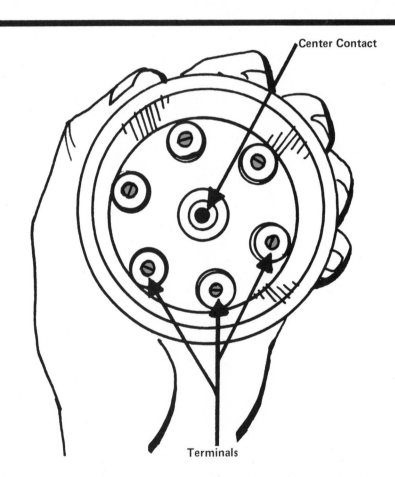

Center Contact

Terminals

When you look inside the distributor cap, you'll see a metal spike for each wire connection and a black "button" made of carbon under the center tower. Look for signs of burned or corroded metal spikes, a deteriorated carbon button, corrosion inside the cap towers or any other signs of cracks or damage to the inside of the cap.

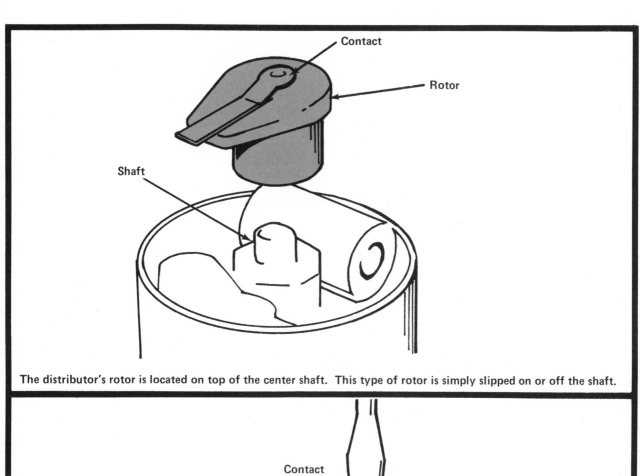

The distributor's rotor is located on top of the center shaft. This type of rotor is simply slipped on or off the shaft.

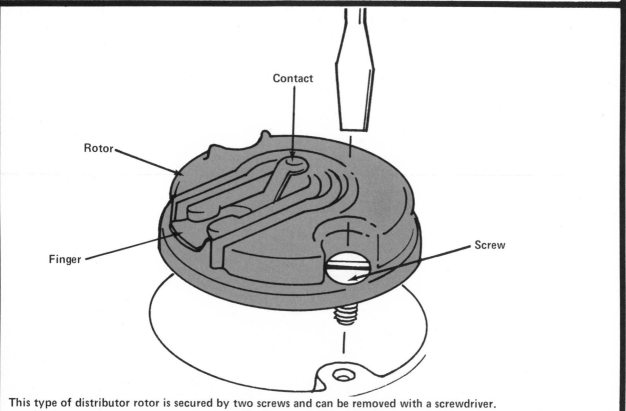

This type of distributor rotor is secured by two screws and can be removed with a screwdriver.

simply slipped onto the shaft so that it can be lifted off with your hand. Perform the following steps:

1. Remove the rotor and inspect it for carbon tracks, cracks or signs of other damage, including any signs of burning on the metal finger on top of the rotor, a bent or broken contact spring, or cracked or broken positioning lug. If you find any of these conditions, the rotor must be replaced.

2. If the cap and rotor pass inspection, clean them with a wiping cloth dampened with a solvent such as alcohol. Don't try to clean the rotor terminal with a file because this will alter the rotor air gap.

3. Wiggle the center shaft of the distributor with your hand. It should be secure. If it's loose, the distributor must be replaced. This is a job for a professional mechanic.

RADIO FREQUENCY INTERFERENCE (RFI) SHIELD. On 1970-73 cars, GM used a radio frequency interference (RFI) shield in the distributors of V8 engines to prevent interference signals from being picked up by a radio antenna in the windshield. If your vehicle has an RFI shield, it's important that there is sufficient space between the ignition point connector and the inside of the shield whenever new breaker points are installed. A piece of insulating tape is applied inside the cover to prevent accidental shortcircuiting. Don't remove this tape!

To service points and condenser on a distributor with an RFI shield, you'll have to remove the shield:

1. Note the position of the two halves of the RFI shield. This will ease reassembly.

2. Remove the two screws holding down the two halves of the shield. The two halves are not interchangeable so they cannot be improperly installed. The shield itself requires no servicing.

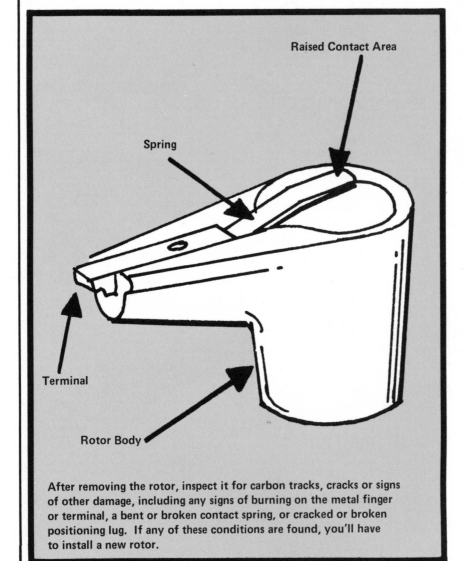

Raised Contact Area

Spring

Terminal

Rotor Body

After removing the rotor, inspect it for carbon tracks, cracks or signs of other damage, including any signs of burning on the metal finger or terminal, a bent or broken contact spring, or cracked or broken positioning lug. If any of these conditions are found, you'll have to install a new rotor.

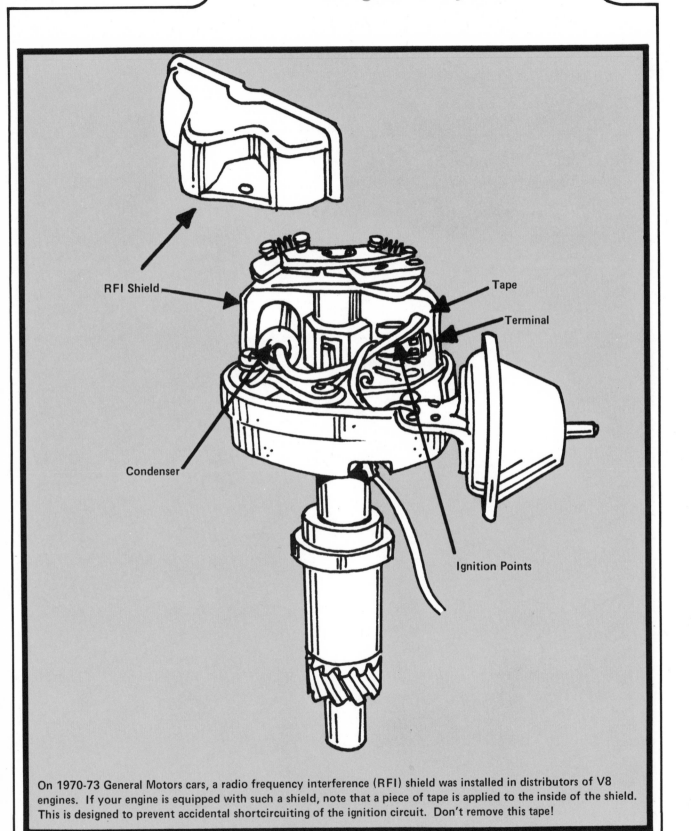

RFI Shield

Tape

Terminal

Condenser

Ignition Points

On 1970-73 General Motors cars, a radio frequency interference (RFI) shield was installed in distributors of V8 engines. If your engine is equipped with such a shield, note that a piece of tape is applied to the inside of the shield. This is designed to prevent accidental shortcircuiting of the ignition circuit. Don't remove this tape!

POINTS AND CONDENSER. Beginning in 1974, GM breaker point distributors for V8 engines use points and condenser called a Uniset assembly. Distributors with the one-piece Uniset points and condenser don't have an RFI shield because their construction eliminates radio interference.

A Uniset assembly can be installed in pre-1974 distributors with no modifications. And, if this is done, the RFI shield can be discarded. It's also possible to install conventional points and a separate condenser in a distributor originally equipped with a Uniset assembly. This can usually be done with no modifications except that, in some cases, it may be necessary to drill and tap a mounting hole for the condenser in the distributor breaker plate. If conventional points and condenser are installed in place of a Uniset assembly,

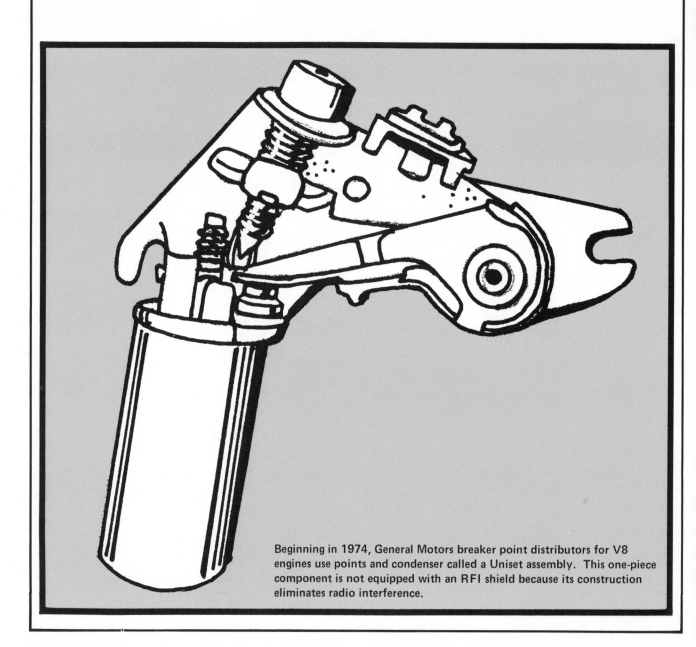

Beginning in 1974, General Motors breaker point distributors for V8 engines use points and condenser called a Uniset assembly. This one-piece component is not equipped with an RFI shield because its construction eliminates radio interference.

an RFI shield must also be installed. Follow these steps to service the points and condenser:

1. After removing the RFI shield (if there is one), inspect the breaker points for pitting and misalignment. Points which are not badly burned or otherwise damaged could be reinstalled, but the point faces must be lightly buffed or burnished to a shiny finish with an ignition point file and properly aligned so that the contacts are flat against each other. In this case, however, we'll replace the points and condenser. So remove them to clean the distributor.
2. Disconnect the wires attached to the movable arm of the breaker points. Use either a wrench or screwdriver, whichever is applicable, to loosen the fasteners and disconnect the two wires. On GM cars with a one-piece points-condenser set, the condenser is removed with the points so only the primary wire needs to be removed.
3. Remove the breaker points.

On GM and AMC V8 engines, use a screwdriver to loosen the two screws holding the points. The points can be removed without removing the screws entirely.

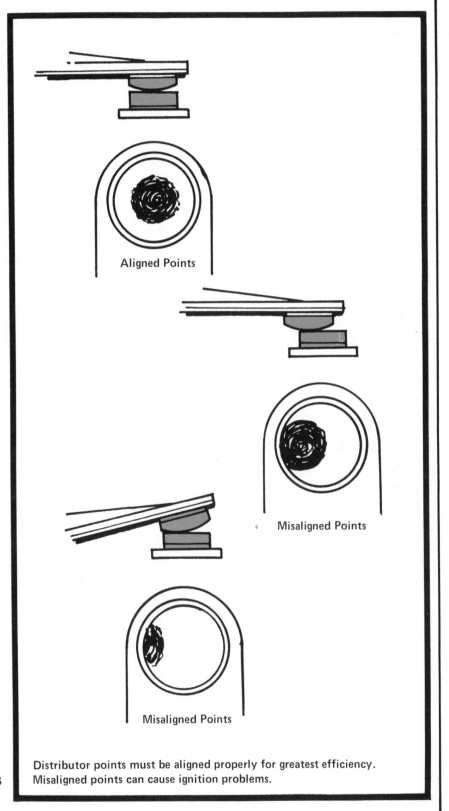

Aligned Points

Misaligned Points

Misaligned Points

Distributor points must be aligned properly for greatest efficiency. Misaligned points can cause ignition problems.

On Ford V8 engines, remove the two screws that hold the points and lift them out.

On Chrysler V8 engines, remove the single screw and lift the points over the locating pin.

Most foreign and other domestic cars will have two screws that hold the points to the distributor breaker plate.

4. Remove the condenser mounting screw that holds the condenser in place, but remember in which direction the wire lead faces for easier reinstallation.

5. Remove the condenser. If the distributor has a cam lubricator or wick under the rotor, remove it too. Look into the distributor for any signs of rust, corrosion, oil or grease. Use a clean cloth soaked with solvent to clean inside the distributor housing and shaft, removing all varnish and gum deposits. Clean any grease and dust from the breaker plate located at the base of the distributor and the distributor cam with a clean wiping cloth. Dry the entire assembly thoroughly.

6. Check any wires and connections inside the distributor and look for

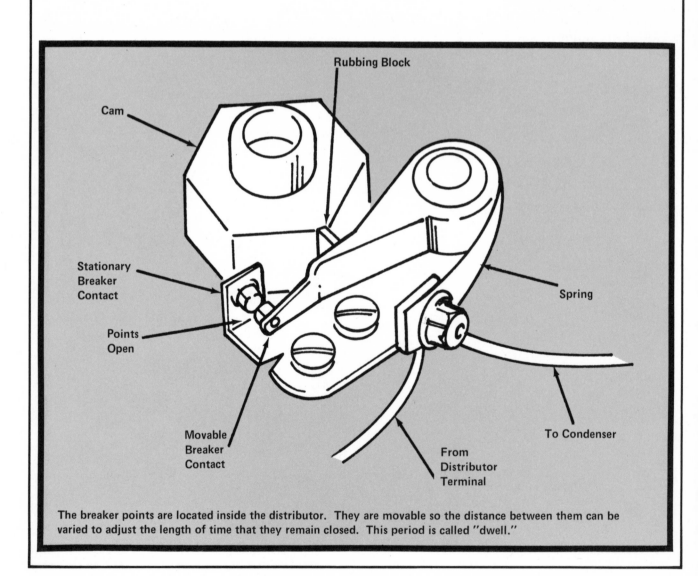

Cam

Rubbing Block

Stationary Breaker Contact

Points Open

Movable Breaker Contact

Spring

To Condenser

From Distributor Terminal

The breaker points are located inside the distributor. They are movable so the distance between them can be varied to adjust the length of time that they remain closed. This period is called "dwell."

signs of deteriorated wire insulation and loose connections. If necessary, replace any wires. Since these internal distributor wires are usually held in place with very small nuts, small open-end ignition wrenches will be required.

7. Lubricate the distributor cam with a light coating of high-temperature grease called cam lubricant. Using the wrong grease can promote varnish and gum deposits and collect dirt. Some replacement points are packed with a small amount of the proper grease for this purpose. Otherwise, you can purchase a small tube of lubricant. Be sure to keep the lubricant off the points, cap, rotor and all electrical connections.

8. Check the new points and condenser you plan to install to make sure that you have the correct replacement parts.

9. Install the points and condenser by reversing Step 2.

On Ford, Chrysler, GM, and AMC six-cylinder engines, don't tighten the points mounting screws until the points have been gapped.

Screws on GM and AMC V8 engines, however, may be tightened because the adjustment is made with a hex-head screw that is part of the points assembly.

If it's not part of a set, install the new condenser, positioning it so the condenser lead end is flush with its mounting bracket to take the slack out of the lead. Then, tighten the bracket hold-down.

NOTE: Some distributors have a felt wick lubricator under the rotor that requires only a few drops of ordinary motor oil. After the points are installed and gapped, apply distributor cam lubricant sparingly to the lobes or high points of the

cam or install a new cam lubricator. Lubricate the breaker point pivot with one drop of oil or a light film of lubricant whenever you replace the points.

If your distributor has a solid cap—one without a window-like opening for adjusting the points—you can proceed to the next section "Gapping the Points." If, however, your distributor has a window for adjusting the breaker points, you can reassemble the distributor at this time. If

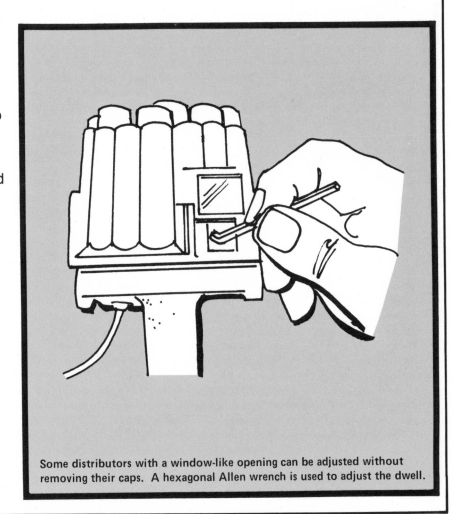

Some distributors with a window-like opening can be adjusted without removing their caps. A hexagonal Allen wrench is used to adjust the dwell.

this is the case, do the following:

1. If you have removed an RFI shield, reinstall it at this time but make sure that the primary or condenser leads are not caught under the edge of the shield before tightening the two shield retaining screws. Failure to install the shield will result in radio interference.

2. Wipe the distributor cam with a clean cloth and apply a film of cam lubricant. If a cam lubricator is used, turn it around to expose fresh lubricant to the cam, or replace the lubricator.

3. Reinstall the rotor. If your rotor was secured by two screws, place the rotor on the distributor shaft. There will be a round and a square peg on the rotor that will fit into a round and square hole in the rotor mount. Don't try to force the rotor. You will break it. Using a screwdriver, tighten the screws. If your rotor simply slips over the distributor's center shaft, you should note a flat side on the shaft. This will correspond to the flat area inside the rotor. It, too, will only go on the shaft one way.

4. Replace the distributor cap, reversing the procedure used for removal.

Gapping the Points.
Correct ignition point alignment and spring tension are essential for proper ignition operation and long service life. Points are correctly aligned when the mating surfaces are in the center of both contacts, the faces are parallel, and the diameters are concentric. This provides maximum contact area and

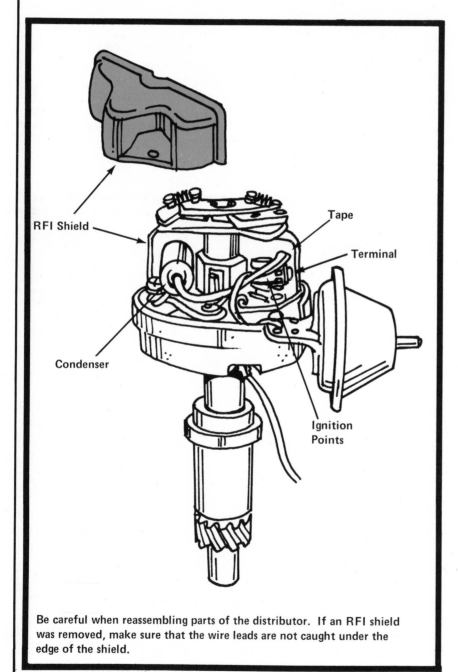

RFI Shield

Tape

Terminal

Condenser

Ignition Points

Be careful when reassembling parts of the distributor. If an RFI shield was removed, make sure that the wire leads are not caught under the edge of the shield.

precise switching action by the points.

Correct spring tension also ensures precise point action. Excessive tension causes rapid distributor cam and rubbing block wear and, in some cases, distributor bushing wear. If the spring tension is too light, the points will bounce as they open and close at high speed. This causes the engine to misfire, resulting in a loss of engine power.

Most replacement ignition points are available in preassembled sets. With these, the point alignment and spring tension will have been set at the factory. Generally, preassembled point sets don't require alignment, but should be checked and aligned if necessary when installed. Dwell adjustment is usually the only adjustment required for preassembled points.

Some replacement points that come as a two-piece set may need alignment and a spring tension adjustment as well as the normal dwell adjustment. Spring tension can be measured with several types of spring scales made for this purpose. Consult the manufacturer's specifications for the proper tension. Don't let the scale arm rub the distributor housing, however, when checking spring tension because this will cause a false reading. Spring tension is generally adjusted by moving an elongated notch in the end of the spring back

and forth on the spring retainer.

If required, point alignment may be adjusted with a special aligning tool. When making this adjustment, never bend the movable contact arm. Bend the stationary contact support to correct the alignment.

SETTING NEW POINTS WITHOUT A DWELL TACHOMETER. New, properly aligned points can be gapped or set with

reasonable accuracy using only a feeler gauge. Used points, however, *must* always be adjusted using a dwell meter. Follow these steps to set new points without a dwell tachometer:

1. Align the points by having someone crank the engine with the ignition switch until the rubbing block on the points assembly is exactly on the peak or high point of one of the distributor cam lobes. The ignition switch

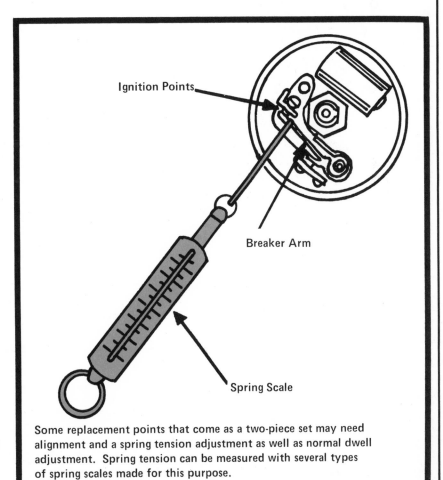

Some replacement points that come as a two-piece set may need alignment and a spring tension adjustment as well as normal dwell adjustment. Spring tension can be measured with several types of spring scales made for this purpose.

should be flicked on just to slightly bump the engine to get the proper point-cam position.
NOTE: Remember to turn the ignition switch *off* once this position has been obtained.
2. Check the specifications for the precise opening required for the points. It will be listed in your service manual. This information is given in thousandths of an inch. For example, 0.017 inch.
NOTE: Some tune-up charts give no specification for ignition point gap. However, there will always be a specification for dwell. If the point gap specification is not known, divide the dwell value by two and the result will be the

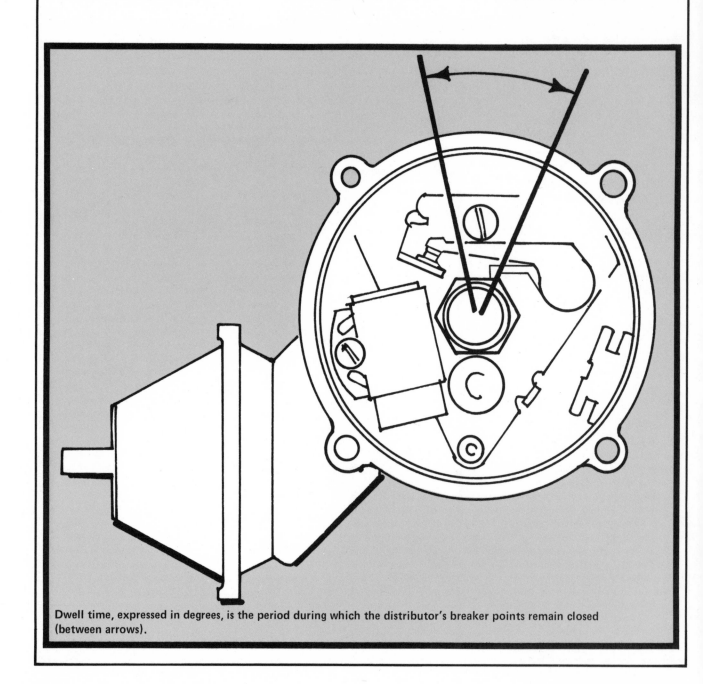

Dwell time, expressed in degrees, is the period during which the distributor's breaker points remain closed (between arrows).

approximate point opening. For example, if the dwell specification is 30, the point opening should be set at fifteen thousandths of an inch (0.015).

CAUTION: Some GM and AMC cars are equipped with ignition breaker points that cannot be set by using a flat feeler gauge. Points of this type have a bimetal saddle installed between the movable (spring-loaded) arm and stationary (ground) arm of the points assembly. Don't attempt to remove the saddle in order to insert a feeler gauge between the contact points. If your car is so equipped, a dwell tachometer *must* be used to establish the point setting.

3. Slide the clean feeler gauge between the points and carefully move the stationary base of the points to adjust the opening. Using a screwdriver, turn the adjusting screw, or open or close the adjusting slot, to obtain the correct opening. A slight drag should be felt as the gauge is drawn between the points and there is no perceptible point movement.
4. Once the gap is set, tighten the points assembly hold-down screws and recheck to make sure the gap hasn't changed.
5. If you have removed an RFI shield, reinstall it at

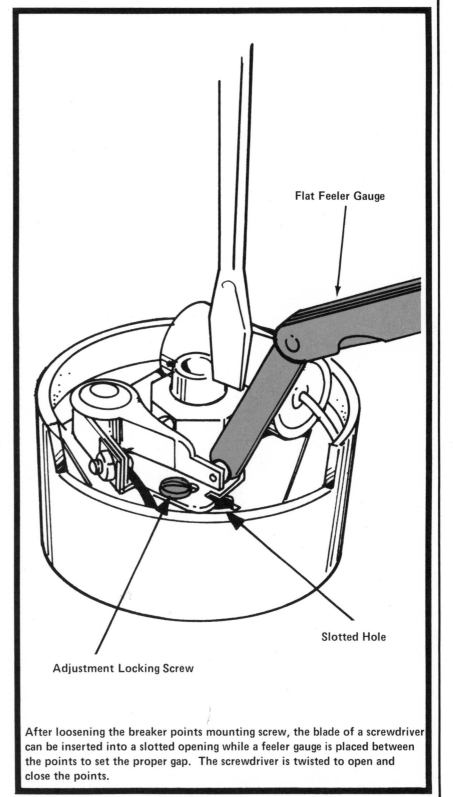

Flat Feeler Gauge

Slotted Hole

Adjustment Locking Screw

After loosening the breaker points mounting screw, the blade of a screwdriver can be inserted into a slotted opening while a feeler gauge is placed between the points to set the proper gap. The screwdriver is twisted to open and close the points.

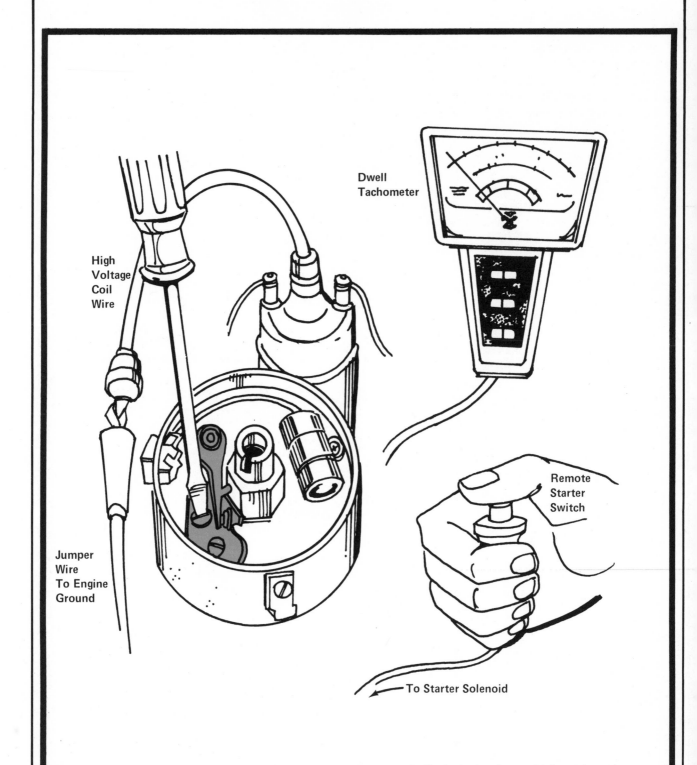

High
Voltage
Coil
Wire

Dwell
Tachometer

Jumper
Wire
To Engine
Ground

Remote
Starter
Switch

To Starter Solenoid

To adjust dwell on a solid-cap distributor, the ignition switch is turned off, the high voltage wire from the ignition coil is grounded to a metal part of the engine with a jumper wire, and vacuum lines are disconnected and plugged. A remote starter switch and a dwell tachometer are also connected.

this time but make sure that the primary or condenser leads are not caught under the edge of the shield before tightening the two shield retaining screws. Failure to install the shield will result in radio interference.

6. Reinstall the rotor. If your rotor was secured by two screws, place the rotor on the distributor shaft. There will be a round and a square peg on the rotor that will fit into a round and square hole in the rotor mount. Don't try to force the rotor. You will break it. Using a screwdriver, tighten the screws. If your rotor simply slips over the distributor's center shaft, you should note a flat side on the shaft. This will correspond to the flat area inside the rotor. It, too, will only go on the shaft one way.

7. Replace the distributor cap, reversing the procedure used for removal.

SETTING POINTS WITH A DWELL TACHOMETER. The dwell angle of a breaker-point distributor is the number of degrees of distributor rotation during which the points stay closed. Dwell adjustment is one of the most important parts of distributor service, and dwell is adjusted by changing the point gap. A smaller gap increases the dwell; a larger gap

decreases the dwell. Dwell can be adjusted by setting the point gap with a feeler gauge as we just described but only with new, properly aligned points. Used points *must* always be adjusted with a dwell tachometer.

The general procedure for adjusting dwell with a dwell tachometer and with the distributor in the engine depends on the type of distributor you have. There are two basic types—one has a solid cap; the other type has a "window-like" opening for the adjustment.

DWELL ADJUSTMENT: SOLID-CAP DISTRIBUTOR. If your distributor has a solid cap, follow these steps:

1. With the ignition switch in the off position, remove the high voltage coil wire from the distributor cap and ground it to a metal part of the engine with a jumper wire.

2. Disconnect and plug vacuum lines with golf tees if required. If you have a Chrysler distributor, disconnect

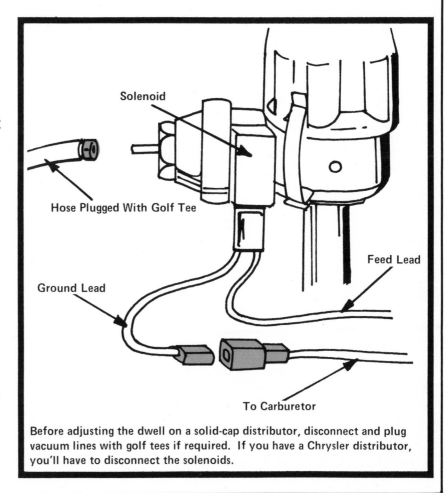

Solenoid

Hose Plugged With Golf Tee

Ground Lead

Feed Lead

To Carburetor

Before adjusting the dwell on a solid-cap distributor, disconnect and plug vacuum lines with golf tees if required. If you have a Chrysler distributor, you'll have to disconnect the solenoids.

The Ignition System

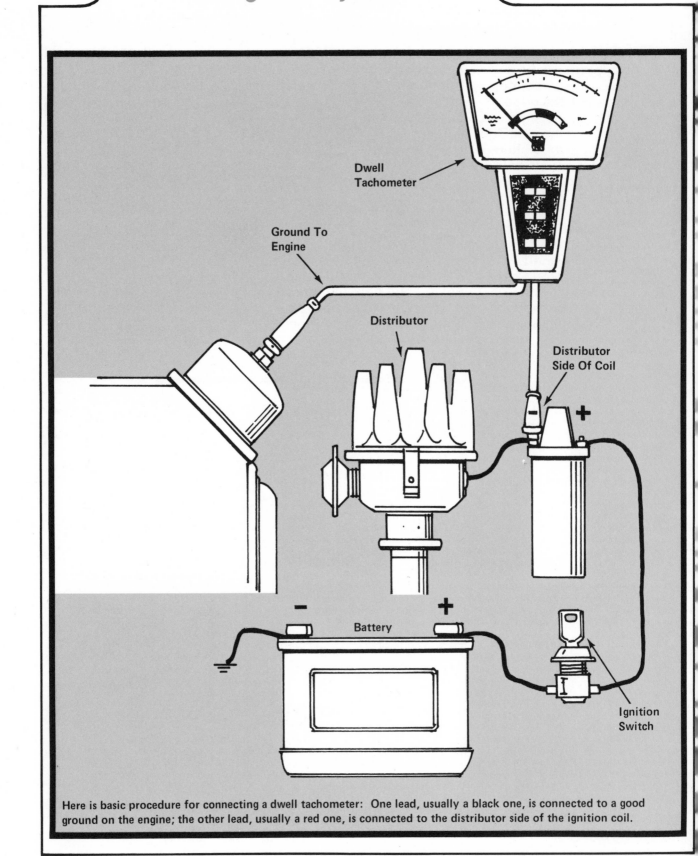

Dwell Tachometer

Ground To Engine

Distributor

Distributor Side Of Coil

Battery

Ignition Switch

Here is basic procedure for connecting a dwell tachometer: One lead, usually a black one, is connected to a good ground on the engine; the other lead, usually a red one, is connected to the distributor side of the ignition coil.

the solenoids.

3. Connect a remote starter switch to the starter solenoid, following the directions supplied with the switch. If you don't have this convenient device, someone will have to assist you by cranking the engine with the ignition switch at certain steps.

4. Connect the dwell tachometer to the engine according to the manufacturer's instructions. The following, however, is a basic procedure for connecting this instrument:

a. On most units, you'll find two wire leads—one red and one black. Connect the black lead to a good ground, such as the negative (−) battery terminal or a part on the engine block. If the leads of your meter have another color code, follow the directions supplied with the unit. **CAUTION:** Never connect the lead to the carburetor or air cleaner stud. This would not only provide a poor ground, but would create a safety hazard—the possibility of electrical sparks near gasoline.

b. Connect the red wire lead to the primary side of the ignition coil. This will be the side to which the distributor breaker points are connected. On some cars,

especially Fords, you will need an adaptor to allow you to connect this lead and still have electrical contact between the coil terminal and the primary lead. These adaptors usually are provided with the test instrument.

5. Turn the ignition to the on position. **CAUTION:** This is important! Failure to do so can result in damage to the ignition switch ground circuit.

6. Loosen the point adjusting screw or shift point bracket with a screwdriver.

7. While observing the dwell tachometer, crank the engine with the remote starting switch. Turn the point adjusting screw or shift point bracket to obtain specified degrees of dwell. Some points are adjusted by turning an eccentric adjustment screw; others are adjusted by moving the mounting bracket with a screwdriver placed in a slotted hole.

8. After adjusting the dwell, retighten the point lock or retaining screws and turn the ignition to the off position.

9. If you have removed an RFI shield, reinstall it at this time but make sure that the primary or condenser leads are not caught under the edge of the shield before

tightening the two shield retaining screws. Failure to install the shield will result in radio interference.

10. Wipe the distributor cam with a clean cloth and apply a film of cam lubricant. If a cam lubricator is used in the distributor, turn it to expose fresh lubricant to the cam, or replace the lubricator.

11. Reinstall the rotor. If your rotor was secured by two screws, place the rotor on the distributor shaft. There will be a round and a square peg on the rotor that will fit into a round and square hole in the rotor mount. Don't try to force the rotor. You will break it. Using a screwdriver, tighten the screws. If your rotor simply slips over the distributor's center shaft, you should note a flat side on the shaft. This will correspond to the flat area inside the rotor. It, too, will only go on the shaft one way.

12. Replace the distributor cap, reversing the procedure used for removal.

13. Reconnect the high voltage coil and remove the jumper wire.

14. Remove the remote starter switch.

DWELL ADJUSTMENT: WINDOW-CAP DISTRIBUTOR. GM V6 and V8 breaker-point distributors have "windows" in their caps so that the dwell angle can be adjusted with the distributor cap in place and with the engine running at idle speed.

NOTE: If your vehicle has a window-cap distributor, proceed to the next section on "Installing the Spark Plugs" *BEFORE* adjusting the dwell.

After the spark plugs have been installed, follow these steps:

1. Connect the dwell tachometer to the engine according to the manufacturer's instructions. The following, however, is a basic procedure for connecting this instrument:

a. On most units, you'll find two wire leads—one red and one black. Connect the black lead to a good ground, such as the negative (−) battery terminal or a part on the engine block. If the leads of your meter have another color code, follow the directions supplied with the unit. **CAUTION:** Never connect the lead to the carburetor or air cleaner stud. This would not only provide a poor ground, but would create a safety hazard—the possibility of electrical sparks near gasoline.

b. Connect the red wire lead

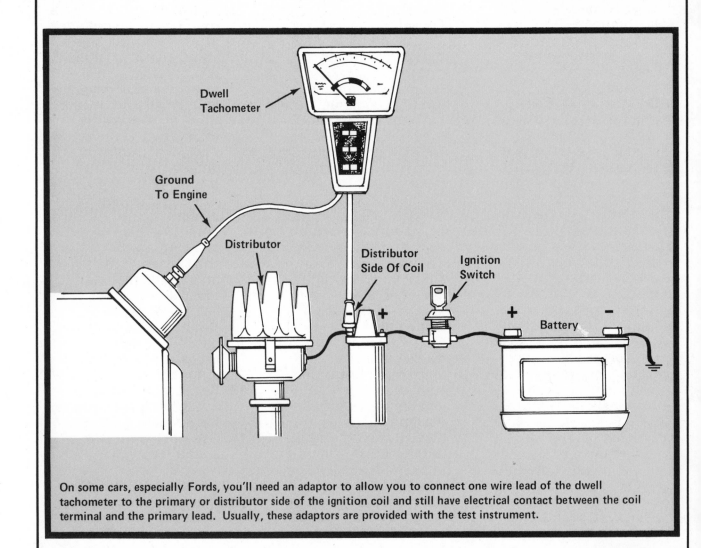

On some cars, especially Fords, you'll need an adaptor to allow you to connect one wire lead of the dwell tachometer to the primary or distributor side of the ignition coil and still have electrical contact between the coil terminal and the primary lead. Usually, these adaptors are provided with the test instrument.

to the primary side of the ignition coil. This will be the side to which the distributor breaker points are connected. On some cars, especially Fords, you will need an adaptor to allow you to connect this lead and still have electrical contact between the coil terminal and the primary lead. These adaptors usually are provided with the test instrument.

2. Start and idle the engine.
3. Raise the window in the distributor cap and insert a hexagonal Allen wrench into the point adjustment screw.
4. While observing the dwell tachometer, turn the adjustment screw clockwise to increase the dwell; counterclockwise to decrease it. The adjustment is self-locking.
5. After the dwell has been adjusted, remove the wrench and close the cap window.

Installing the Spark Plugs. After the points have been gapped and the dwell has been adjusted properly, it's time to install the used spark plugs that have been cleaned and gapped, or the new plugs whose gaps have been set correctly. (If you have a window-cap distributor, install the spark plugs *before* setting the dwell.)

For this, you will need the following tools and materials: clean cloths,

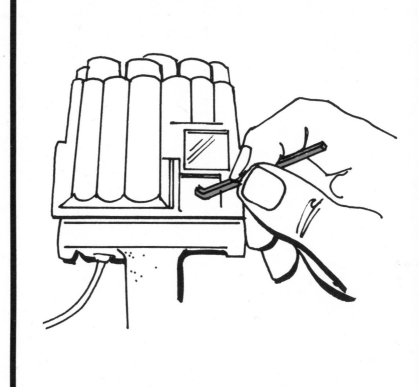

To adjust dwell on a window-cap distributor, turn the adjustment screw clockwise to increase the dwell; counterclockwise to decrease it. The adjustment is self-locking.

penetrating oil, a short length of scrap heater hose, torque wrench (optional), and spark plug socket and ratchet wrench. Follow these steps:

1. Wipe any remaining dirt and grease from the plug seats in the engine with a dry clean cloth.
2. Be sure that the metal gaskets on gasketed plugs are in good condition and are properly seated on the plugs.
3. Install the plugs into the

engine finger tight. If you have trouble getting the plugs started in their holes by hand, the threads in the cylinder head may require cleaning. Usually, these threads can be cleaned by applying penetrating oil to them. Soak a corner of a clean cloth with oil. Twist the oil-soaked cloth into the spark plug hole, turning it clockwise. Remove the cloth by turning it counter-clockwise. Repeat as often as is required to remove the dirt. If the threads are clean and you still have trouble, try slipping the end of a short length of scrap heater hose over the end of the plug to form a flexible handle.

NOTE: Be careful when you install spark plugs in aluminum cylinder heads. The threads in these heads are easily damaged if the spark plug is installed under heavy force. A thin coating of anti-seize compound applied to the spark plug threads will assure proper seating and ease installation.

4. Tighten the plugs with a torque wrench to the foot-pound values shown in the accompanying table. If a torque wrench is not available, use a spark plug ratchet and socket and give each finger-tight plug another quarter to half turn, making it snug but not too tight! If your car uses tapered plugs, which do not have gaskets, there will be a metal-to-metal contact so only about a quarter turn is required for a proper seal.
5. Reconnect each spark plug cable to the proper plug. Push the wire's rubber boot firmly over the tip of the plug with your hand. Remove from the cables any labels made with masking tape.

Checking the Dwell Setting. If you have a

Spark Plug Torque Specifications		
Plug Thread Size	**Iron Head**	**Aluminum Head**
14mm, gasketed	25-30 lb. ft.	18-22 lb. ft.
14mm, tapered	7-15 lb. ft.	7-15 lb. ft.
18mm, tapered	15-20 lb. ft.	15-20 lb. ft.

distributor with the solid cap, start and idle the engine. Check the dwell setting, and readjust it if required. If you have a distributor with the window-like opening, you already have checked the dwell setting.

Timing the Engine. One of the most troublesome components in a car's ignition system always has been the distributor's breaker points. Today, however, the points and condenser of conventional systems have been replaced in most new automobiles by electronic ignition systems, which cause far fewer problems. With such systems, virtually no maintenance is required for 30,000 miles or more. Both the convention breaker-point and electronic ignitions, however, must be timed. General procedures for both types are covered.

CONVENTIONAL IGNITIONS. After ignition breaker points are installed

in a distributor, the engine must be timed. The purpose is to ensure that each spark plug will fire at exactly the right moment for maximum engine efficiency. The spark occurs in microseconds and is measured in terms of degrees before top dead center (BTDC) in relation to each piston as it goes through its cycle.

Most engines have the basic timing index in the form of a line, dent, etc., that is marked on the rim of the engine's vibration damper. This is the heavy steel wheel that is connected to the crankshaft at the front of the engine. Some engines will have several marks on the vibration damper and a single pointer on the timing cover. Others will have only one mark on the damper and a plate extending from the timing cover with several divisions indicating varying degrees of engine timing. Timing is set by aligning two of these points while the engine is running.

The timing is generally set

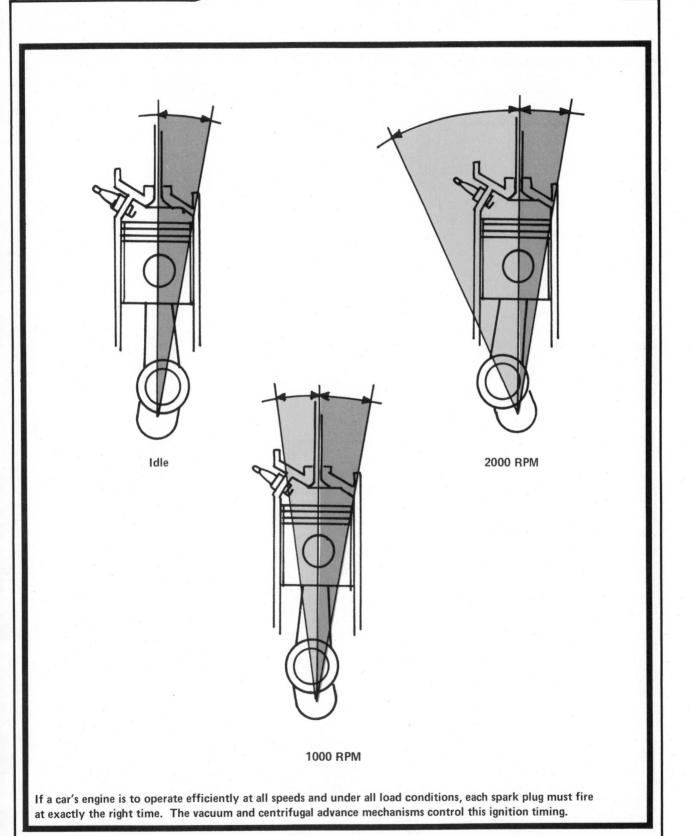

Idle

1000 RPM

2000 RPM

If a car's engine is to operate efficiently at all speeds and under all load conditions, each spark plug must fire at exactly the right time. The vacuum and centrifugal advance mechanisms control this ignition timing.

by using a strobe lamp—a light that is operated by high voltage surges from the No. 1 spark plug wire. After the basic contact point gap (or dwell) is accurately set, the strobe lamp is connected to a power source and to the No. 1 spark plug wire. The engine is started and idled slowly. Usually, the vacuum line to the vacuum advance unit at the distributor is removed and plugged with a golf tee.

The strobe light is aimed so that it shines on the pointer over the vibration damper. Each time the No. 1 spark plug fires, the strobe lamp will light. Since the spark plug fires with the damper in the same position in relation to the pointer, the timing marks will appear to be standing still.

ALTERNATE TIMING-LIGHT HOOKUPS. Because of options such as air conditioning and pollution control devices that are mounted on engines, it may be difficult to connect a timing light to the No. 1 spark plug. There is, however, a way around this problem—alternate timing. Simply stated, correct timing can be obtained by the "companion cylinder method." This also applies to electronic ignition timing.

This method allows you to hook the timing light to a spark plug other than the No. 1 cylinder and still set the proper basic timing. **NOTE:** This tip only applies to engines with an *even*

number of cylinders and will not work on exotic three- and five-cylinder engines.

The companion cylinder to No. 1 can be quickly determined by the engine's firing order as follows:

In a four-cylinder engine, the companion cylinder is the third cylinder in the firing order.

In a six-cylinder engine, the companion cylinder is the fourth cylinder in the firing order.

In an eight-cylinder engine, the companion cylinder is the fifth cylinder in the firing order.

Firing order can be found by either looking at the engine's intake manifold where it will be stamped into the metal, or by consulting tune-up specifications in your service manual.

For timing your engine, you'll need the following items: a timing light, clean cloths, chalk, golf tees, and a socket extension and ratchet wrench or a distributor wrench.

To set basic timing, follow these steps:

1. With the engine off, clean the timing marks on your engine with a clean rag.
2. On the clean surface, put a chalk mark on the two points that you want to align in the timing process. Check the service manual timing specifications for your engine. On late-model engines, the timing

setting is provided on an engine tune-up data decal in the engine compartment.

3. Connect a timing light to your engine. With a direct current (DC) timing light, the black lead wire is connected to the negative (−) terminal on your battery. The red lead wire is connected to the positive (+) terminal. With an alternating current (AC) timing light, these connections are not necessary because the light draws its power from a 110-volt source (drop light, extension cord, etc.). In either case, there is an additional wire or lead from the timing light. This is connected to the No. 1 spark plug or to the spark plug wire of the No. 1 cylinder of your engine. Adaptors to make this connection come with the timing light. Refer to the tune-up guide in your service manual for the location of the No. 1 cylinder on your engine.

NOTE: If you are planning to buy a timing light, try to get one with the type of lead that gets its impulse signal from a clamp-on connection at the spark plug wire. This greatly simplifies the operation. This is called an inductive-pickup timing light. In any case, *never* puncture a spark plug cable or boot with a sharp probe to connect a timing light!

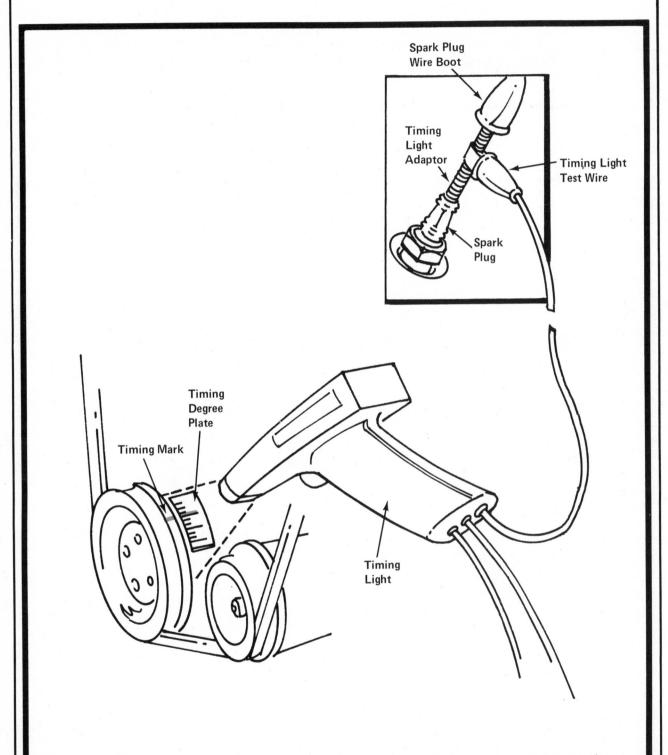

Spark Plug
Wire Boot

Timing
Light
Adaptor

Timing Light
Test Wire

Spark
Plug

Timing
Degree
Plate

Timing Mark

Timing
Light

With a direct current timing light, the black lead wire is connected to the negative terminal of the battery; the red wire lead is connected to the positive terminal. The light's third wire is connected to the No. 1 spark plug or to the spark plug wire of the No. 1 cylinder. Adaptors to make this connection come with the timing light.

4. On some engines the vacuum is left connected during timing, but for most it is disconnected and plugged. If this is the case, locate the distributor's vacuum advance unit. Disconnect the rubber vacuum hose by pulling it off the unit and plugging the hose with a golf tee. A vacuum leak here will cause the engine to run rough, and a true timing check will not be possible. On dual- diaphragm distributors, the vacuum

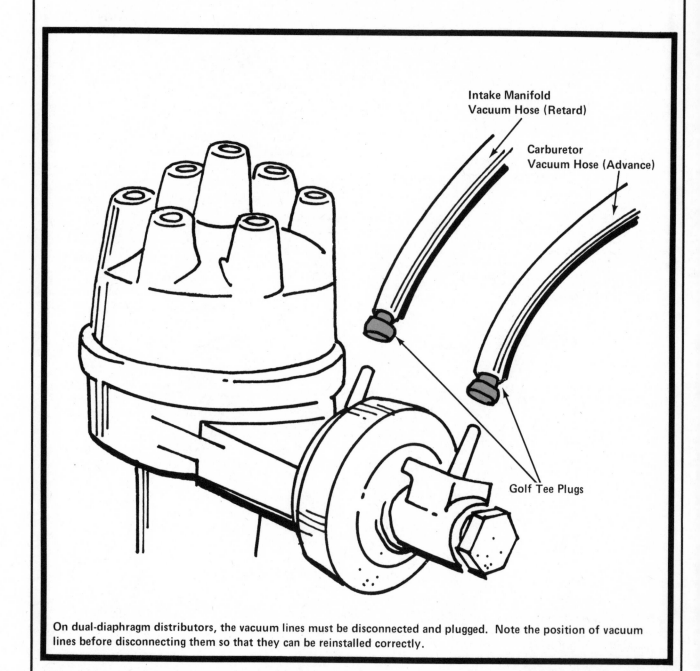

Intake Manifold Vacuum Hose (Retard)

Carburetor Vacuum Hose (Advance)

Golf Tee Plugs

On dual-diaphragm distributors, the vacuum lines must be disconnected and plugged. Note the position of vacuum lines before disconnecting them so that they can be reinstalled correctly.

lines must be disconnected and plugged. Note the position of vacuum lines before disconnecting them so that they can be reinstalled correctly.

5. Make sure all wires are clear of the engine fan.

6. Start the engine and let it run at idle speed. The dwell must be adjusted and the engine must be at its normal operating temperature before timing is adjusted, so run the engine for about 15 minutes to reach normal operating temperature.

7. Point the light at the timing marks on the crankshaft pulley, being careful to keep the light and your hands away from the engine fan. If the chalk marks are lined up, your engine is properly timed and you may proceed to Step 11. If they are not lined up, proceed to the next step.

8. With the engine still running, loosen the distributor hold-down bolt found at the outside base of the distributor where it attaches to the engine. This bolt actually holds a bracket that keeps the distributor in place. You will need a socket extension and ratchet wrench for this task.

9. Now with the engine running and the activated timing light pointing at the timing marks, carefully rotate the distributor a fraction of an inch at a time—clockwise or counterclockwise—until the timing marks line up. Rotate it *against* rotor rotation to advance the timing; *with* rotor rotation to retard the timing. The engine is now basically timed.

10. Retighten the distributor hold-down bolt. Recheck the timing after you have tightened the bolt to be sure that the distributor has not moved.

11. Remove the golf tee and reconnect the distributor vacuum advance rubber hose. Proceed to "Spark Advance Mechanisms."

ELECTRONIC IGNITION. Advantages of electronic ignition systems are: there is more available secondary circuit voltage to reduce engine misfiring; less spark plug fouling, hence longer plug life; less high-speed missing to improve fuel economy and reduce emissions; and more reliable starting.

Although the differences between an electronic ignition system and the conventional point system it replaces are great, there are few differences in servicing. Fortunately, most of these differences make the task easier.

In electronic ignition systems, for example, the distributor cam is replaced by a round part with teeth that resembles a pointed wheel. Chrysler calls this device a "reluctor," Ford calls it an "armature," and General Motors calls it a "timing core." Ford's name probably comes closest to describing the part's function, so "armature" is the term we use here.

Along with the armature is a magnetic pickup coil, which replaces the breaker points of a conventional system, and a transistorized control box. As the distributor shaft turns, the teeth of the armature pass the pickup coil and establish a magnetic impulse that then is directed to a control module. The control module is designed to break the coil's primary circuit each time an impulse is received from the pickup coil. Breaking of the coil's primary circuit will allow the coil's secondary circuit to produce the high voltage necessary to fire the spark plug.

Electronic ignitions can raise voltage to the spark plugs up to 40,000 volts as compared with 15,000 to 20,000 volts in conventional systems. With this greater voltage, spark plugs can be gapped wider for better performance. This high voltage, however, imposes greater demands on spark plug wiring. So, you must be sure that the wires' insulation is in good shape and that all connections are clean and tight. Also, you must check the distributor cap and rotor for cracks, dirt and corrosion.

As stated earlier, there are significant differences between electronic and conventional ignition systems. There are also significant differences between the electronic ignition systems as used by the various car manufacturers, so it is important to take a look into some of the systems used and how they can be serviced.

Recently built Chrysler engines are equipped with an electronic ignition system having a special distributor with no ignition points or cam. Instead, a rotating reluctor transmits a timing pulse to a magnetic pickup coil and then to an electronic control unit. Voltage to fire spark plugs is interrupted by the transistorized control unit each time an impulse is received. The system may be recognized by a double-wire primary lead between the distributor and the ignition coil.

There are two basic types of transistorized systems. One operates on the magnetic pulse principle with no ignition points. The second type uses ignition points to control a transistorized circuit in which current is limited to about 0.5 ampere. Point arcing is reduced, thus prolonging point life. When used, systems are identified by engine applications in your tune-up specifications.

A unit ignition system is used on some General Motors' engines. All components of the system—magnetic pickup coil, timer core that provides centrifugal advance, vacuum advance unit, electronic module, rotor, and ignition coil—are assembled into the unit distributor. The system may be recognized by the larger, unconventional shape of the distributor. Beginning in 1975, an improved version of the unit distributor was introduced and used as standard equipment on all General Motors' vehicles. It is referred to as the High Energy Ignition (HEI) system.

Capacitive discharge systems are primarily produced by "after-market" manufacturers. The system is designed to maintain a constant secondary (high voltage) output, despite primary voltage fluctuations. Often referred to as CD ignition, the system is visually identifiable by a small external control unit connected by wires to the distributor and by the letters "CD" marked on it.

ELECTRONIC IGNITION TIMING. To time an electronic ignition, refer to the illustrations of timing mark locations at the beginning of tune-up specifications in the service manual for your car. Timing is set before top dead center (BTDC); at top dead center (TDC) or after top dead center (ATDC). Top dead center represents zero degrees. Some timing mark scales are marked "A" (advance) or "R" (retard), corresponding to settings before or after top dead center. For this operation, you'll need the following: a timing light, dwell tachometer, golf tees, clean cloths, and a socket extension and ratchet wrench. Follow these procedures for setting basic ignition timing on vehicles equipped with electronic ignition systems:

1. Run the engine until it reaches normal operating temperature (about 15 minutes) and stop it.
2. Connect a timing light to the engine. With a direct current (DC) timing light, the black lead wire is connected to the negative (−) terminal on your battery. The red lead wire is connected to the positive (+) terminal. With an alternating current (AC) timing light, these connections are not necessary because the light draws its power from a 110-volt source (drop light, extension cord, etc.) In either case, there is an additional wire or lead from the timing light. This is connected to the No. 1 spark plug or the spark plug wire of the No. 1 cylinder of your engine. Adaptors to make this connection come with the timing light. Refer to the tune-up guide in your

service manual for the location of the No. 1 cylinder on your engine.

NOTE: Check special instructions for setting timing given in your tune-up specification.

3. Connect a dwell tachometer, which

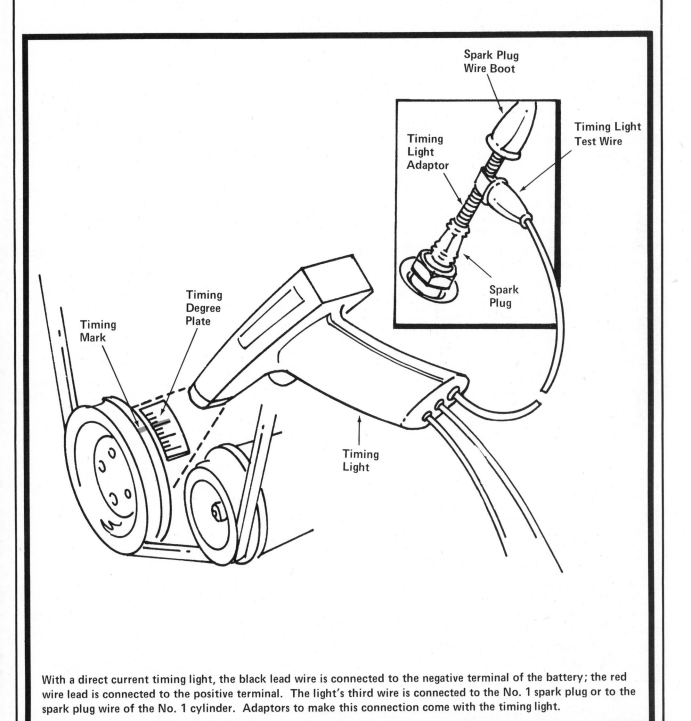

Spark Plug Wire Boot

Timing Light Test Wire

Timing Light Adaptor

Spark Plug

Timing Mark

Timing Degree Plate

Timing Light

With a direct current timing light, the black lead wire is connected to the negative terminal of the battery; the red wire lead is connected to the positive terminal. The light's third wire is connected to the No. 1 spark plug or to the spark plug wire of the No. 1 cylinder. Adaptors to make this connection come with the timing light.

measures revolutions per minute (rpm), to the engine. This instrument has two lead wires. Connect the black lead to any metal part of the engine, such as a bolt head or bracket to ground it. Connect the red lead wire to the distributor side of the ignition coil.

4. If the car has a vacuum-operated parking brake, disconnect it and plug the hose from the power unit with a golf tee to prevent a vacuum leak.

5. Loosen the distributor hold-down bolt at the base of the distributor where it attaches to the engine. You will need a socket extension and a ratchet wrench for this task.

6. Start and idle the engine or set it to the rpm specified in your service manual.

7. Aim the timing light at the stationary mark or pointer while turning the distributor housing slowly until the rotating mark is aligned with the stationary mark. Refer to the cylinder number sequence illustrations in your service manual. Turning the distributor housing clockwise retards spark timing; turning it counterclockwise advances spark timing.

8. When the two marks are aligned, retighten the distributor bolt and recheck the timing.

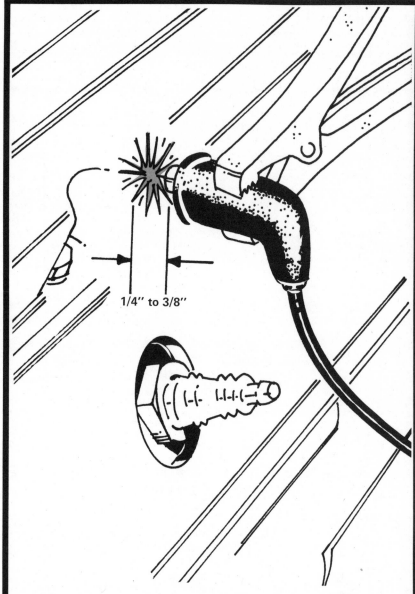

1/4″ to 3/8″

To determine if starting problems are caused by a bad electronic ignition system, remove the wire from a spark plug and hold it about 1/4 inch from the engine with a pair of insulated pliers. If a spark jumps from the wire to the engine when the engine is cranked, you'll know the electronic ignition system is not the cause of the problem.

9. Readjust engine rpm, if necessary, to specified idle speed and stop the engine.

10. Disconnect the tachometer.

11. Reconnect any disconnected hoses.

NOTE: On point-controlled transistorized ignition systems, the ignition timing must always be checked and reset if necessary after distributor dwell angle has been adjusted.

The ignition timing on some imported cars is set statically (with the engine not running) using a test lamp. Specific procedures, where applicable, will be given in tune-up specifications in your service manual.

Ignition timing on some 1972-77 Ford-built engines for California cars is factory-set with an electronic system known as monolithic timing. A magnetic pickup attached to the engine transmits a timing impulse to an instrument meter indicating spark firing.

SPARK ADVANCE MECHANISMS. Setting the engine's basic ignition timing, whether you have a conventional or electronic system, only assures you that the timing is correct at one speed. If an automobile engine is to operate efficiently at all speeds and under all load conditions, it is essential for each spark plug to fire at exactly the right time. As engine speed and load change, so does the ignition timing requirement. It's not practical to manually change timing during engine operation, so distributors are equipped with automatic advance mechanisms.

To achieve maximum efficiency, there are two devices in the distributor to control ignition timing under various speed and load conditions—the vacuum advance unit and the centrifugal advance

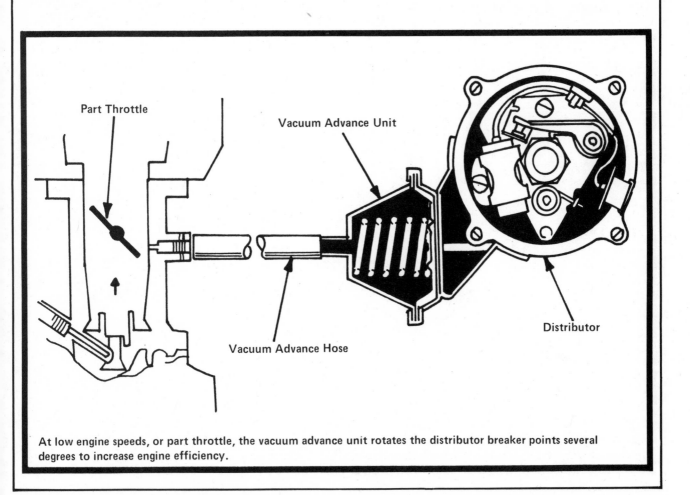

Part Throttle

Vacuum Advance Unit

Vacuum Advance Hose

Distributor

At low engine speeds, or part throttle, the vacuum advance unit rotates the distributor breaker points several degrees to increase engine efficiency.

mechanism. Although some distributors have only one or the other, most distributors have both.

It is necessary for these mechanisms to be operating properly to obtain maximum fuel economy. Therefore, a check of those units should be included in each tune-up. You'll only need a timing light and some golf tees.

CHECKING VACUUM ADVANCE. To check vacuum advance, follow this procedure:

1. With the engine running, quickly unplug and reconnect the vacuum line to the distributor. Check the basic timing mark location with the timing light. You should find that the timing mark has advanced several degrees away from BTDC. **NOTE:** If no timing advance has occurred, check for vacuum leaks at the line connections or a cracked vacuum line. If this is not the problem, the vacuum advance unit is defective and must be replaced.

2. With the timing light aimed at the timing marks, note the position of the marks. Next, reach over and quickly open the throttle. If this is not physically possible, have someone sit in the car and sharply depress the accelerator pedal, releasing it immediately. You should see the timing marks return to almost the initial timing setting and then return to the first observed position before the throttle was opened. This is due to the sudden decrease in manifold

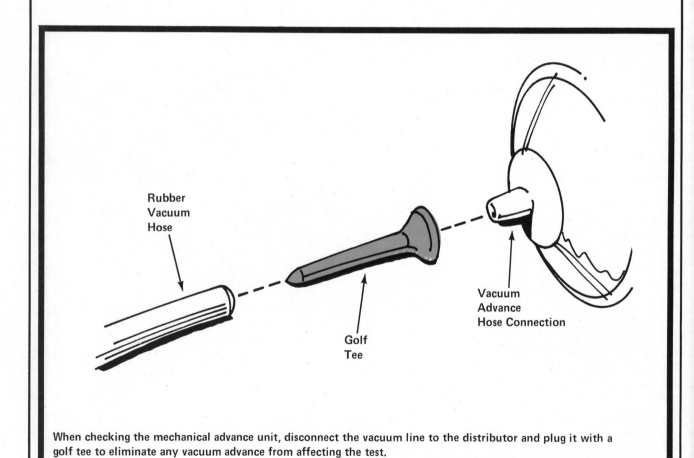

Rubber Vacuum Hose

Golf Tee

Vacuum Advance Hose Connection

When checking the mechanical advance unit, disconnect the vacuum line to the distributor and plug it with a golf tee to eliminate any vacuum advance from affecting the test.

vacuum when the throttle was opened. The decreased vacuum allows the return spring in the vacuum advance unit to move the distributor points breaker plate in a "retard" direction. If the timing marks did not appear to move, the breaker plate may be binding inside the distributor housing, or the return spring in the vacuum advance unit is too weak. Repair of the distributor or replacement of the vacuum advance unit will be necessary. If the described results were obtained, the vacuum advance unit is functioning properly.

3. Stop the engine.

Next, you should check another important timing advance mechanism, the centrifugal advance unit.

CHECKING CENTRIFUGAL ADVANCE. Unlike the vacuum advance unit, which responds to engine load conditions, the centrifugal advance mechanism responds to engine speed. The specific engine speed at which mechanical advance will begin varies widely. On some foreign cars—Opel, for example—the initial mechanical advance may begin as low as 150 rpm. On most domestic cars, measurable mechanical advance begins at about 1000 rpm.

The mechanical advance unit reacts during

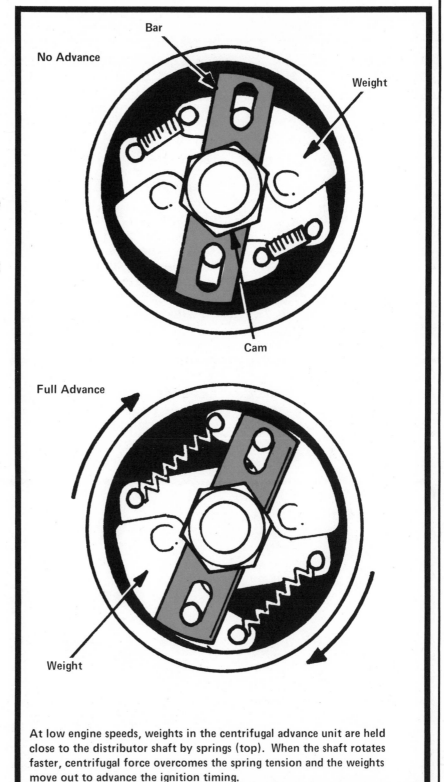

At low engine speeds, weights in the centrifugal advance unit are held close to the distributor shaft by springs (top). When the shaft rotates faster, centrifugal force overcomes the spring tension and the weights move out to advance the ignition timing.

acceleration and higher engine rpm. During acceleration, manifold vacuum drops, but additional advance is needed to accommodate the normal richer air/fuel mixture. Because engine speed is increasing, there is less time for the power stroke to take place. Therefore, the spark must occur earlier to burn the mixture effectively.

High intake manifold vacuum present during cruising speeds also requires additional ignition advance. Because of the shorter period in which combustion takes place, timing advance supplied by the vacuum advance unit is insufficient. Here's where the mechanical unit helps. The effects of the vacuum and mechanical advance units are cumulative.

Since the vacuum unit moves the entire breaker plate mechanism, mechanical advance can still occur. In essence, vacuum and mechanical advance are compounded to advance timing to a degree much higher than either the vacuum or mechanical units could create separately.

Here is how to check your mechanical advance unit:

1. With the timing light still connected, disconnect the vacuum line to the distributor and plug it with a golf tee to eliminate any vacuum advance from affecting the test.
2. Start the engine and increase engine speed while observing the timing marks. You may need someone to help you here too. If the mechanical advance mechanism is functioning properly, the timing will advance (move against engine rotation) as the engine speed is increased above 1000 rpm. The observed timing marks should appear to move as engine speed is changed. If they don't, then the unit is defective and professional help is required to correct it.
3. Stop the engine and disconnect the timing light. Remove the golf tee and reconnect the vacuum line.

TIMING TEST WITHOUT A POWER TIMING LIGHT. Even if your timing light doesn't have a timing

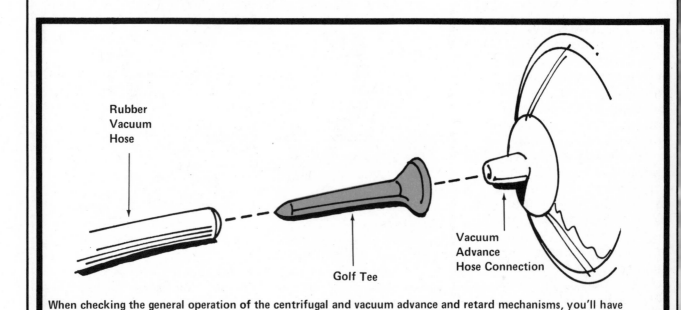

Rubber Vacuum Hose

Golf Tee

Vacuum Advance Hose Connection

When checking the general operation of the centrifugal and vacuum advance and retard mechanisms, you'll have to disconnect and plug the distributor vacuum lines with golf tees.

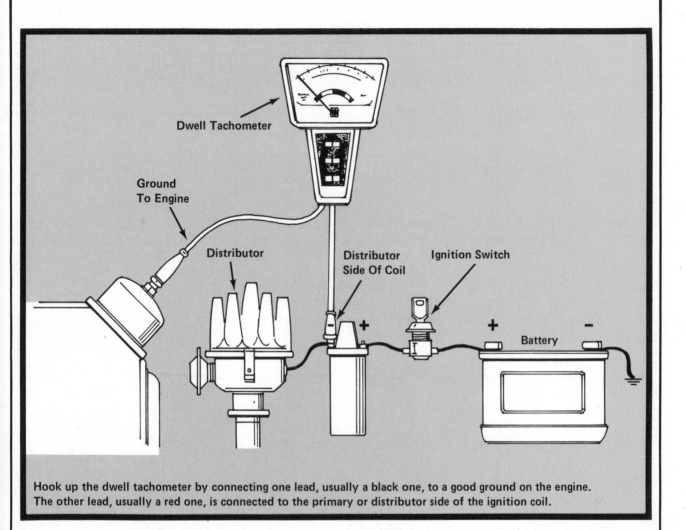

Dwell Tachometer

Ground To Engine

Distributor

Distributor Side Of Coil

Ignition Switch

Battery

Hook up the dwell tachometer by connecting one lead, usually a black one, to a good ground on the engine. The other lead, usually a red one, is connected to the primary or distributor side of the ignition coil.

advance meter, the general operation of the centrifugal and vacuum advance and vacuum retard mechanisms can be checked. To do so, follow these steps:

1. Connect a dwell tachometer and timing light.
2. Start and idle the engine.
3. Disconnect and plug the distributor vacuum lines with golf tees.
4. Accelerate the engine to 2000 or 2500 rpms while observing the timing marks. The marks should advance smoothly and steadily, indicating that the centrifugal advance is working.
5. While holding the engine speed at 2000 or 2500 rpm, unplug and connect the vacuum advance line to the distributor.
6. The timing marks should advance an additional amount and engine speed should increase, indicating that the vacuum advance is working.
7. Check vacuum retard on dual-diaphragm distributors by connecting the manifold vacuum line to the retard chamber with the engine at idle. Timing should retard approximately 6 to 12 degrees, and engine speed should decrease.
8. Stop the engine and disconnect the dwell tachometer and the timing light.

Adjusting the Carburetor

The carburetor is a most important part of the fuel system. It's a simple device that has the job of automatically vaporizing a small quantity of gasoline and mixing it with a large volume of air. When drawn into the engine, this highly combustible mixture is exploded by the spark plugs and power is developed to move the car.

The carburetor consists of three basic parts: the tube, called the air horn, through which air from the air cleaner is drawn; a damper, called a butterfly or throttle valve, that can be opened or closed to regulate the passage of air through the air horn; and a nozzle through which gasoline is

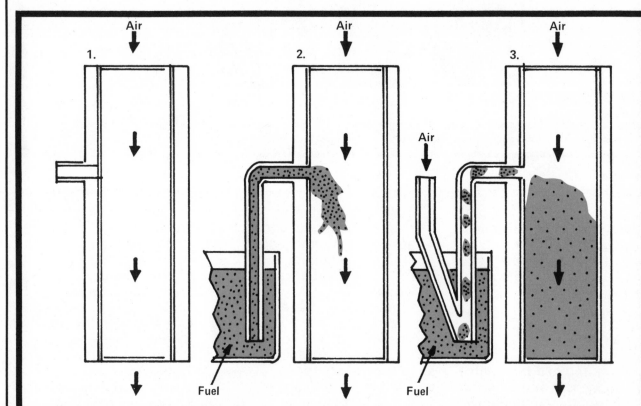

A carburetor operates on the Venturi principle. Air rushing down a large tube will draw air through a small tube in its side (1). If the small tube leads to a container of fuel, incoming air will draw fuel into the large tube (2). A "V" in the small tube allows an air/fuel mixture to flow into the large tube.

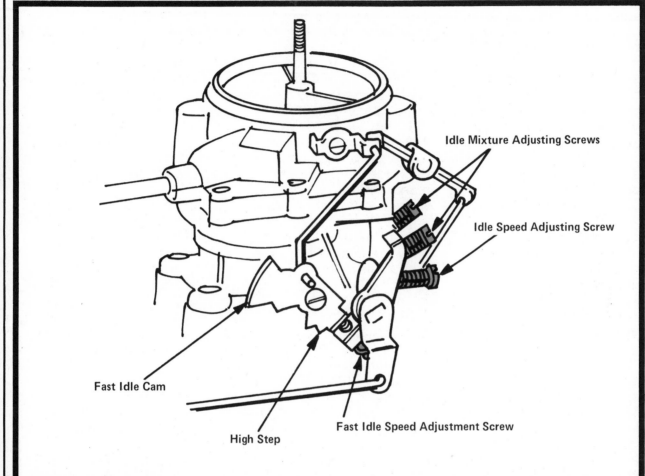

Idle Mixture Adjusting Screws

Idle Speed Adjusting Screw

Fast Idle Cam

Fast Idle Speed Adjustment Screw

High Step

Idle mixture adjusting screws can be turned clockwise or counterclockwise to make the air/fuel mixture leaner or richer. The idle speed adjusting screw is used to increase or decrease the engine's rpm.

drawn into the air horn. The throttle butterfly valve, however, should not be confused with the choke valve which is located in the top section of the carburetor. Varying the throttle opening allows regulated amounts of this air/fuel mixture to be drawn into the engine's cylinders, which causes variations in engine speed and power.

If the throttle valve is closed all the way, the engine will not run. A means of keeping the valve from closing all the way is located in the throttle linkage on the outside of the carburetor. This part of the linkage is called the idle speed adjusting screw, or throttle stop screw. By turning this screw in (clockwise), the engine idle speed is increased. By turning it out (counterclockwise), engine idle speed is decreased. The adjustment of the idle screw simply regulates the closing position of the throttle valve inside the carburetor and should not be confused with the idle mixture adjusting screws. **NOTE:** Some carburetors are equipped with an anti-dieseling solenoid. This unit operates as part of the throttle stop linkage and must be considered when adjusting engine idle speed.

Depending on the size of the carburetor, there will be one or two idle mixture screws located in its base casting. The idle mixture screw is a simple valve that regulates the amount of gasoline being mixed with the air flowing through the carburetor at low engine speeds. If the idle mixture screw is turned in (clockwise), the gasoline flow is reduced and the air/fuel mixture becomes "lean." When the idle mixture screw is turned out (counterclockwise), the flow of gasoline is increased and the air/fuel mixture becomes "rich."

Basically, these adjustments are intended to correct two minor faults that detract from driving pleasure. However, they also are important final steps to every complete tune-up.

The need for carburetor adjustment can be identified by the following symptoms:

If the idle speed is adjusted too low, the engine will stall when the car is slowed to a stop or when the transmission is shifted into gear.

When the idle speed is adjusted too high, the engine will tend to diesel or run on after the ignition is switched off.

An engine that is operating with the idle air/fuel mixture too lean may hesitate on acceleration and run roughly at idle speed.

An idle air/fuel mixture that is too rich causes excessive use of fuel and high exhaust emissions.

Engine faults traced to the wrong idle speed or idle air/fuel mixture can be easily corrected by following the procedures outlined in this section. But, before you begin making adjustments, it is a good idea to check the information that the car manufacturer has posted in various locations in the engine compartment in the form of decals or stickers. They are helpful because they contain specific servicing information.

Adjusting the Idle Speed. Depending on the type of car you have, the idle speed is adjusted either by means of an idle speed screw or by an idle solenoid and set screw. Consult your service manual or the tune-up decal in the engine compartment if you are in doubt as to which adjustment you have. Also, check to determine at what speed your engine should idle and if adjustments should be made with the transmission in drive or not, or if any electrical accessories should be switched on or off. Power from the engine is used to drive these components and their use places a load on the engine that affects the idle speed.

For example, shifting an automatic transmission into drive range takes power from the engine and results in lowering the idle speed. Also, turning on accessories such as air conditioning adds to the engine load. These power-using loads must be taken into consideration when the engine idle speed needs to be adjusted.

Because the carburetor air cleaner housing blocks your view of the linkage and adjusting screws, it should be removed. It's good practice to make the initial adjustments with the air cleaner housing removed and any final adjustment with it installed.

Manufacturer's instructions for carburetor idle speed and mixture adjustments vary. However, you should observe these basic guidelines:

- The car's entire ignition system must be in proper operating condition before adjusting the carburetor.
- The fuel pump must deliver fuel at the right pressure.
- The engine must be at normal operating temperature (warmed up for about 15 minutes) and the choke must be open.
- The parking brake must be set and the drive wheels blocked.

For adjusting the carburetor, you'll need the following: wheel chocks, golf tees, wrench, dwell tachometer, and a screwdriver.

IDLE SPEED SCREW ADJUSTMENT. If your

Before beginning to adjust the idle speed, make sure that the car's parking brake is set and the vehicle's drive wheels are blocked with wheel chocks.

carburetor has an idle speed screw, here is how to make the idle speed adjustment:

1. Make sure that the parking brake is set and the wheels are blocked with wheel chocks.
2. Start the engine and allow it to reach normal operating temperature (about 15 minutes).
3. Stop the engine and remove the air cleaner housing. **NOTE:** Any vacuum hoses that have been removed from the air cleaner housing must be plugged. A golf tee is a good plugging tool. Vacuum lines that are left open will affect the engine idle speed.
4. Connect a dwell tachometer to the engine. The instrument has two lead wires—one red, one black. Connect the black lead to any metal part of the engine, such as a bolt head or bracket, to ground it. Connect the red lead to the ignition coil at the wire lead that runs to the distributor.
5. Start the engine.
6. Set the transmission and any accessories according to instructions on the tune-up decal or directions in your owner's manual.
7. Observe the meter reading. Compare the indicated speed with the recommended speed. If adjustment is necessary, proceed to the next step. If no adjustment is required, go to Step 9.
8. Using a screwdriver, turn the idle speed set screw clockwise to increase rpm, counterclockwise to decrease rpm. You will find that a ¼ turn of the screw in either direction will usually bring the idle speed into specification.
9. Stop the engine.
10. Reinstall the air cleaner housing, but leave the dwell tachometer hooked up.

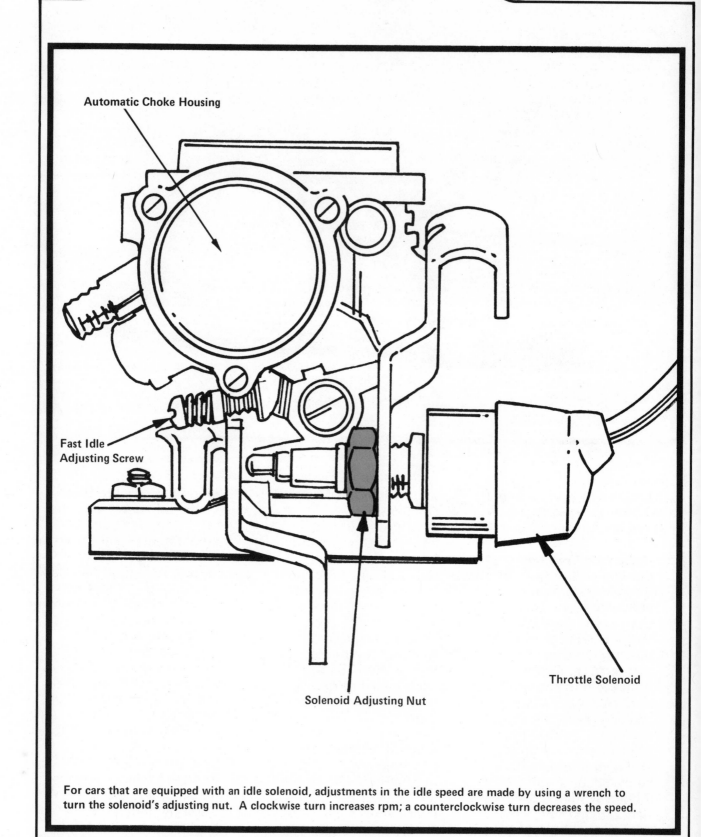

Automatic Choke Housing

Fast Idle
Adjusting Screw

Solenoid Adjusting Nut

Throttle Solenoid

For cars that are equipped with an idle solenoid, adjustments in the idle speed are made by using a wrench to turn the solenoid's adjusting nut. A clockwise turn increases rpm; a counterclockwise turn decreases the speed.

11. Start the engine and check the meter reading. If it is within specification (plus or minus 20 rpm), proceed to the idle air/fuel adjustments. If it is not, adjust the idle speed set screw carefully to bring the idle speed into specification.

IDLE SOLENOID AND SET SCREW ADJUSTMENT. If your carburetor is equipped with an idle solenoid and set screw, here is how to make the idle speed adjustments:

1. Make sure that the parking brake is set and the wheels are blocked with wheel chocks.
2. Start the engine and allow it to reach normal operating temperature (about 15 minutes).
3. Stop the engine and remove the air cleaner housing. **NOTE:** Any vacuum hoses that have been removed from the air cleaner housing must be plugged. A golf tee is a good plugging tool. Vacuum lines that are left open will affect the engine idle speed.
4. Connect a dwell tachometer to the engine. The instrument has two lead wires—one red, one black. Connect the black lead to any metal part of the engine, such as a bolt head or bracket, to ground it. Connect the red lead to the ignition coil at the wire that leads to the distributor.
5. Start the engine.
6. Set the transmission and any accessories according to instructions on the tune-up decal or directions in your owner's manual.
7. Observe the meter reading. Compare the indicated speed with the recommended speed. If adjustment is necessary, proceed to the next step. If no adjustment is required, go to Step 9.
8. To make the solenoid rpm adjustment, use a wrench to turn the solenoid adjusting nut clockwise to increase rpm, counterclockwise to decrease rpm. Adjust until the specified rpm is reached.
9. To make the base idle or slow idle rpm adjustment, disconnect the solenoid wire at the spade or bullet connector. This will cause the solenoid plunger to retract and the rpm will be reached.
10. Observe the meter. If the indicated speed is at or near 500 rpm, no adjustment is required. If it is not, use a screwdriver to turn the base idle screw until the meter indicates 500 rpm.
11. Reconnect the solenoid wire.
12. Depress the accelerator or move the carburetor throttle linkage by hand to increase the engine rpm. This will allow the solenoid plunger to extend to the position of the first adjustment. Release the pressure on the linkage so the engine rpm will come back to idle speed.
13. Observe the meter reading. It should be at the specification you set in Step 8. If it is not, make the adjustment at this time.
14. Stop the engine.
15. Reinstall the air cleaner housing, but leave the meter hooked up.
16. Start the engine and check the meter reading. If the reading is within specification (plus or minus 20 rpm) proceed to the next step. If it is not, make a final adjustment at this time.
17. Stop the engine.

Adjusting Idle Air/Fuel Mixture. To make the idle air/fuel mixture adjustments, follow these steps:

1. Start the engine.
2. Set the transmission and any accessories according to the tune-up decal or directions in your owner's manual.
3. Locate the idle air/fuel mixture screws. **NOTE:** Single-barrel carburetors have one adjusting screw; two- and four-barrel carburetors have two adjusting screws.
4. Note the rpm indicated on the dwell tachometer. Using a small screwdriver, carefully turn the adjusting screw in (clockwise) until the

Adjusting the Carburetor

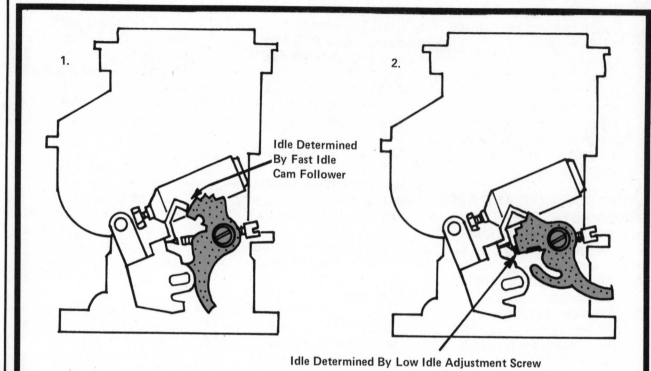

1.

Idle Determined
By Fast Idle
Cam Follower

2.

Idle Determined By Low Idle Adjustment Screw

3.

Idle Determined By Plunger

Here is how linkage is activated by the anti-dieseling solenoid: The choke is on and the solenoid is energized (1). The choke is off and the solenoid is de-energized (2). The choke is off and the solenoid is energized (3).

engine falters and there is a drop in rpm. When the engine falters, this condition is called the lean roll rpm. Now turn the adjusting screw out (counterclockwise) until the engine speed reaches its highest rpm. This point is said to be the optimum or balanced rpm, and the engine should run very smoothly. If your carburetor has two mixture adjusting screws, adjust them both in the manner just described. **NOTE:** Your carburetor may have plastic limiter caps covering the heads of the adjusting screws. These limiter caps, which restrict the amount of possible adjustment to one turn or less, should not be removed. To do so is a violation of federal and state pollution control laws.

5. Stop the engine.

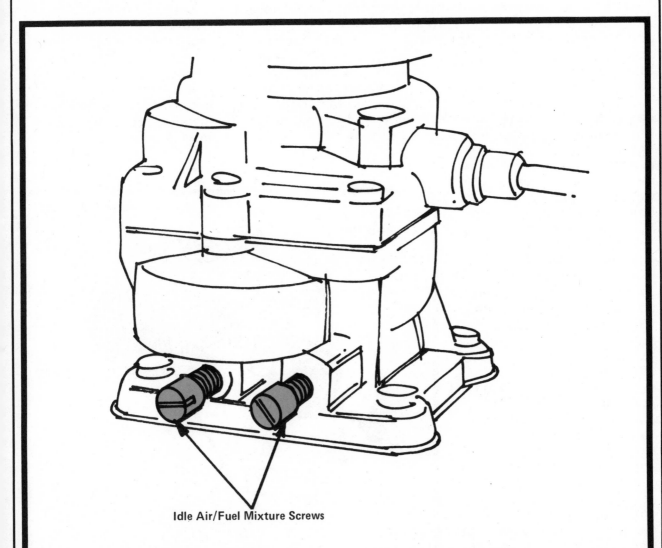

Idle Air/Fuel Mixture Screws

A two- or four-barrel carburetor has two idle air/fuel mixture screws. They are turned right or left to adjust the engine's idle speed. A clockwise turn decreases the speed: a counterclockwise turn increases engine rpm.

Final Tune-Up Steps

Now that the battery, spark plugs and other ignition system components have been checked and serviced, and the carburetor has been correctly adjusted, you're ready to complete the final steps in the tune-up.

During any tune-up, the operation of the manifold heat control valve should be checked. Thermostatic heat control valves, controlled by a spring and a counterweight, should be checked for free movement by pressing on the counterweight. This check, however, should be done with the engine off. If a valve is stuck, it can often be freed by tapping it with a hammer while applying some valve solvent to the valve. Periodically, the valve shaft should be lubricated with special solvent. Don't apply motor oil to a heat control valve. Because the valve is exposed to hot exhaust, oil will carbonize and cause sticking.

Vacuum-operated heat control valves should be checked for proper diaphragm operation and for free movement of the valve. Apply some vacuum to the diaphragm and watch for linkage movement.

Thermostatic vacuum switches and vacuum solenoids that control valve operation should also be tested for correct operation.

Finally, inspect the engine compartment to see that every component has been replaced and fastened properly, and that no tools or other objects have been left inside the engine compartment.

Then, close the hood, gather up your tools, and store them. Remove the chocks from the drive wheels and you should be ready for many miles of better performance and increased fuel economy from your car.

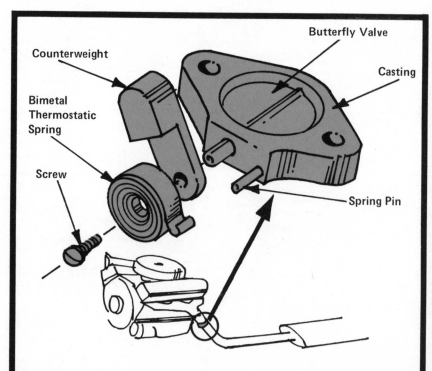

Counterweight
Butterfly Valve
Casting
Bimetal Thermostatic Spring
Screw
Spring Pin

Deposits could cause the manifold heat control valve to stick and the engine to vapor lock or falter on acceleration. It's a good idea to check this valve when performing a tune-up.

QUICK-REFERENCE MAINTENANCE AND LUBRICATION GUIDE*

* Service intervals may vary according to manufacturer's make and model.

Service at Indicated Time and/or Mileage Intervals	Fuel Stop	2 Months		6 Months		12 Months		24 Months
		2000 Miles	4000 Miles	5000 Miles	6000 Miles	10000 Miles	12000 Miles	24000 Miles
Check Engine Oil Level	•							
Check Radiator Coolant Level	•							
Check Battery Liquid Level	•							
Check Windshield Washer Reservoir Level	•							
Lubricate Generator Cup(s) (if so equipped)		•						
Lubricate Distributor Cup		•						
Lubricate Water Pump (if equipped with grease fittings)		•						
Change Engine Oil and Filter (Capacity)			•					
Check Tire Air Pressure (Front Rear)			•					
Lubricate Front Suspension (# of points)			•					
Lubricate Exhaust Manifold Valve			•					
Check Brake Master Cylinder Fluid Level			•					
Check Hydraulic Clutch Master Cylinder Fluid Level			•					
Check Automatic Transmission Fluid Level			•					
Check Power Steering Fluid Reservoir			•					
Check Steering Gear Lubricant Level			•					
Clean & Lubricate Oil Wetted Wire Mesh Air Cleaner*			•					
Clean & Lubricate Oil Filler Cap*			•					
Check and Clean Crankcase Ventilation System					•			
Check Manual Transmission Lubricant Level (early type)					•			
Check Manual Transmission Lubricant Level (full syncro type)							•	
Check Rear Axle Lubricant Level (early)					•			
Check Rear Axle Lubricant Level (late)								•
Lubricate Transmission, Brake & Clutch Linkage					•			
Adjust Clutch Pedal Travel					•			
Lubricate Universal Joints W/Grease Fittings					•			

Continued on Next Page

QUICK-REFERENCE MAINTENANCE AND LUBRICATION GUIDE*
(Continued)

* Service intervals may vary according to manufacturer's make and model.

Service at Indicated Time and/or Mileage Intervals	2 Months		6 Months		12 Months		24 Months
	2000 Miles	4000 Miles	5000 Miles	6000 Miles	10000 Miles	12000 Miles	24000 Miles
Lubricate Universal Joints W/o Grease Fittings							●
Perform Brake Adjustment**				●			
Clean Body & Door Drain Holes				●			
Rotate Tires				●			
Clean Dry-Type Air Cleaner*				●			
Replace Dry-Type Air Cleaner*						●	
Clean Polyurethane-Type Air Cleaner*				●			
Perform Body Lubrication (hinges, striker plates, etc.)				●			
Inspect Brake Hoses				●			
Check Accessory Drive Belt Tension				●			
Clean & Refill Oil Bath Type Air Cleaner*					●		
Clean & Lubricate Accelerator Linkage						●	
Lubricate Dash Controls & Seat Tracks						●	
Clean Battery Terminals**						●	
Check Air-Conditioning System (bolts, hose connections, sight glass)						●	
Replace PCV Valves & Clean Hoses						●	
Inspect Cooling System**						●	
Change Automatic Transmission Fluid							●
Check Shock Absorbers & Bushings							●
Lubricate Speedometer Cable							●

* Perform This Service More Frequently In Dusty Areas
** More Frequently If Necessary

Make a note of when each service was last performed and keep an accurate list to avoid future problems.

USE THIS SPACE TO RECORD SPECIFICATIONS FOR YOUR CAR:

PLUG TYPE_____ DWELL_____ DEG. TIMING_____ OIL FILTER_____

Glossary

A

ADVANCE (Ignition timing): To set the ignition timing so that a spark occurs earlier or more degrees before Top Dead Center (TDC).

AUTOMATIC CHOKE: A carburetor choke device that automatically positions itself in accordance with carburetor needs.

B

BDC: Bottom dead center.

BLOW-BY: Refers to the escape of exhaust gases past the piston rings.

BREAKER POINTS: Two points (one movable) in the distributor that, when moved apart, interrupt current flow in the primary circuit.

BUTTERFLY VALVE: A valve in the carburetor that is so named due to its resemblance to the insect of the same name.

C

CAM ANGLE or DWELL (Ignition): The number of degrees the breaker cam rotates from the time the breaker points close until they open again.

CAMSHAFT: A shaft with cam lobes (bumps) used to operate the valves.

CENTRIFUGAL ADVANCE (Distributor): A unit designed to advance and retard the ignition timing through the action of centrifugal force.

CHOKE: A butterfly valve located in the carburetor that is used to enrich the mixture for starting the engine when cold.

CID: Cubic inch displacement.

COIL: A spiral made of wire; a device used in automobiles to increase the voltage to the spark plug, or to provide the electromagnetic force in a solenoid.

COMBUSTION CHAMBER: The area above the piston with the piston on TDC. The head of the piston, the engine cylinder, and the head form the chamber.

COMPRESSION CHECK: Testing the compression in all the cylinders at cranking speed. All plugs are removed, the compression gauge placed in one plug hole, the throttle opened wide and the engine cranked until the gauge no longer climbs. The compression check is a way to determine the condition of the valves, rings and cylinders.

COMPRESSION GAUGE: A gauge used to test the compression in the cylinders.

COMPRESSION RATIO: Relationship between the cylinder volume (clearance volume) when the piston is on TDC and the cylinder volume when the piston is on BDC.

CONDENSER (Ignition): A unit installed between the breaker points and coil to prevent arcing at the breaker points. A condenser has the ability to absorb and retain surges of electricity.

CONTACT POINTS (Breaker points): Two movable points or areas that, when pressed together, complete a circuit. These points are usually made of tungsten, platinum or silver.

CYLINDER: The hole, or holes, in the engine cylinder block that contain the pistons.

CYLINDER HEAD: The metal section that is bolted on top of the block. It is used to cover the tops of the cylinders. In many cases, the cylinder head contains the valves. It also forms part of the combustion chamber.

D

DISCHARGE (Battery): Drawing electric current from the battery.

DISPLACEMENT: The total volume of air displaced by the piston in traveling from BDC to TDC.

DISTRIBUTOR (Ignition): A unit designed to make and break the ignition primary circuit and to distribute the resultant high voltage to the proper cylinder at the correct time.

DISTRIBUTOR CAP (Ignition): An insulated cap containing a central terminal with a series (one per cylinder) of terminals that are evenly spaced in a circular pattern around the central terminal. The secondary voltage travels to the central terminal where it is then channeled to one of the outer terminals by the rotor.

DUAL BREAKER POINTS (Ignition): A distributor using two sets of breaker points to increase the cam angle so that at high engine speeds, sufficient spark will be produced to fire the plugs.

E

ELECTRODE (Spark plug): The center rod passing through the insulator forms one electrode. The rod welded to the shell forms another. They are referred to as the center and side electrodes.

ELECTROLYTE: A solution of sulphuric acid and water used in the cells of a battery to react chemically with the differing materials in the electrodes and produce an electrical current.

ENGINE DISPLACEMENT: The volume of the space through which the head of the piston moves in the full length of its stroke —multiplied by the number of cylinders in the engine. The result is given in cubic inches.

EXHAUST MANIFOLD: Connecting pipes between the exhaust ports and the exhaust pipe.

F

FEELER GAUGE: A thin strip of hardened steel ground to an exact thickness that is used to check clearance between parts.

FIRING ORDER: The order in which cylinders must be fired —1, 5, 3, 6, 2, 4, etc.

FLOODING: A condition where the fuel mixture is overly rich or an excessive amount has reached the cylinders. Starting will be difficult and sometimes impossible until the condition is corrected.

FOOT-POUND: A measurement of the work involved in lifting one pound one foot.
   Also, a one-pound pull one foot from the center of an object.

FUEL MIXTURE: A mixture of gasoline and air. An average mixture, by weight, would contain 16 parts of air to one part of gasoline.

FUEL PUMP: A vacuum device, operated either mechanically or electrically, that is used to draw gasoline from the tank and force it into the carburetor.

G

GAP: The space or "break" in the continuity of a circuit, such as between ignition contact points.

GASKET: A material placed between two parts to insure proper sealing.

GROUND: A condition where the electrical circuit is connected to the unit frame by means of a strap or rod.

H

HEAT RANGE (Spark plug): Refers to the operating temperature of a given style plug. Plugs are made to operate at different temperatures, depending upon the thickness and length of the porcelain insulator as measured from the sealing ring down to the tip.

HEAT RISER: An area surrounding a portion of the intake manifold through which exhaust gases pass to heat the fuel mixture during warm-up.

HYDROMETER: An instrument with a float housed in a glass tube that measures specific gravity of a liquid.

I

IN-LINE ENGINE: An engine in which all the cylinders are arranged in a straight row.

INTAKE MANIFOLD: Connecting tubes between the base of the carburetor and the port openings to the intake valves.

J

JET: A small hole or orifice used to control the flow of gasoline in the various parts of the carburetor.

K

KNOCKING (Fuel): A condition, accompanied by an audible noise, that occurs when the gasoline in the cylinders burns too quickly. This is also referred to as detonation.

L

LINKAGE: A system of links and levers connected together to transmit motion or force.

LUBRICANT: Any material, usually of a petroleum nature such as grease or oil, that is placed between two moving parts in an effort to reduce friction.

M

MANIFOLD HEAT CONTROL VALVE: A valve placed in the exhaust manifold, or in the exhaust pipe, that deflects a certain amount of hot gas around the base of the carburetor to aid in warm-up.

N

NEGATIVE TERMINAL: That terminal (such as that on the battery) from which the current flows on its path to the positive terminal.

O

OIL BATH AIR CLEANER: An air cleaner that utilizes a pool of oil to insure the removal of impurities from air entering the carburetor.

OIL FILTER: A device used to strain the oil in the engine, thus removing abrasive particles.

P

PENETRATING OIL: A special oil that is used to free rusted parts so that they can be removed.

PINGING: A metallic rattling sound produced by the engine during heavy acceleration when the ignition timing is too far advanced for the grade of fuel being burned.

PISTON: A round plug, open at one end, that slides up and down in the cylinder. It is attached to the connecting rod and when the fuel charge is fired, the piston will transfer the force of the explosion to the connecting rod and then on to the crankshaft.

PISTON RING: A split ring installed in a groove in the piston. The ring contacts the sides of the ring groove and also rubs against the cylinder wall, thus sealing the space between the piston and the wall.

Also, a ring designed to seal the burning fuel charge above the piston. Generally, there are two compression rings per piston and they are located in the two top ring grooves.

PLUG GAPPING: Adjusting the side electrode on a spark plug to provide the proper air gap between it and the center electrode.

POSITIVE TERMINAL: The terminal at which electrons enter a battery or a generator.

PRIMARY: The inducing current to the coil windings or capacitor that is the source of the high tension secondary voltage in an ignition system.

R

RESISTOR SPARK PLUG: A spark plug containing a resistor designed to shorten both the capacitive and inductive phases of the spark. This will suppress radio interference and lengthen electrode life.

RETARD (Ignition timing): To set the ignition timing so that a spark occurs later or less degrees before TDC.

ROTOR (Distributor): A cap-like unit placed on the end of the distributor shaft. It is in constant contact with the distributor cap central terminal and as it turns, it will conduct the secondary voltage to one of the outer terminals.

S

SECONDARY CIRCUIT (Ignition system): The high voltage part of the ignition system.

SOLENOID: A tubular coil containing a magnetic core that moves when the coil is energized.

SPARK ADVANCE: Causing the spark plug to fire earlier by altering the position of the distributor breaker points in relation to the distributor shaft.

SPARK PLUG: A device containing two electrodes across which electricity jumps to produce a spark to fire the fuel charge.

STROKE: The distance the piston moves when traveling from TDC to BDC.

T

TACHOMETER: A device used to indicate the speed of the engine in rpm.

TDC: Top dead center.

THROTTLE VALVE: A valve in the carburetor that is used to control the amount of fuel mixture that reaches the cylinders.

TIMING LIGHT: A stroboscope unit that is connected to the secondary circuit to produce flashes of light in unison with the firing of a specific spark plug. By directing these flashes of light on the whirling timing marks, the marks appear to stand still. By adjusting the distributor, the timing marks may be properly aligned, thus setting the timing.

TIMING MARKS (Ignition): Marks, usually located on the vibration damper, used to synchronize the ignition system so that the plugs will fire at the precise time.

TORQUE: Turning or twisting effort measured in foot-pounds or inch-pounds.

TORQUE WRENCH: A special wrench that indicates the amount of torque being applied to a nut or bolt.

TRANSISTOR IGNITION: Form of ignition system that utilizes transistors and a special coil. The conventional distributor and point setup is used. With the transistor unit, the voltage remains constant, thus permitting high engine rpm without the resultant engine "miss." Point life is greatly extended as the transistor system passes a very small amount of current through the points.

TUNE-UP: The process of checking, repairing and adjusting the carburetor, spark plugs, points, belts and timing to obtain the maximum performance from the engine.

V

VACUUM ADVANCE (Distributor): A unit designed to advance and retard the ignition timing through the action of engine vacuum working on a diaphragm.

VAPORIZATION: Breaking the gasoline into fine particles and mixing it with the incoming air.

VAPOR LOCK: Boiling or vaporizing of the fuel in the lines from excess heat. The boiling will interfere with the movement of the fuel and in some cases will completely stop the flow.

VIBRATION DAMPER: A round weighted device attached to the front of the crankshaft to minimize the torsional vibration.